SKETCHES OF SCENERY AND MANNERS
IN THE UNITED STATES

By Theodore Dwight, Jr.

**A PHOTOREPRODUCTION
WITH AN INTRODUCTION BY
JOHN F. SEARS**

SCHOLARS' FACSIMILES & REPRINTS
DELMAR, NEW YORK
1983

SCHOLARS' FACSIMILES & REPRINTS
ISSN 0161-7729
SERIES ESTABLISHED 1936
VOLUME 383

Published by
Scholars' Facsimiles & Reprints
Delmar, New York 12054

New matter in this edition
(C) 1983 Scholars' Facsimiles & Reprints, Inc.

Library of Congress Cataloging in Publication Data

Dwight, Theodore, 1796-1866.
Sketches of scenery and manners in the United States.

Reprint. Originally published:
New York : A.T. Goodrich, 1829.
1. New England--Description and travel--1775-1865.
2. New England--Social life and customs.
3. Education, Preschool--United States--
History--19th century.
4. Nursery schools--New England.
I. Title.
F8.D996   1983   974'.007   82-10258
ISBN 0-8201-1383-2

INTRODUCTION

Sketches of Scenery and Manners in the United
States, by Theodore Dwight, Jr., has not been re-
printed since its original publication in 1829 and
has gone unnoticed by historians of American culture. The obscurity of this interesting and unusual
book may be because it fell outside the mainstream
of nineteenth-century responses to the American
landscape. The primary purpose of the book, unlike
that of most nineteenth-century travel literature,
was to instruct rather than to entertain and inspire, or to promote particular places. Scenery and
Manners reflects the attitude, established in the
eighteenth century, that travel is an important
means of education, but Dwight applies that idea
much more systematically than other travel writers.
He adopts a particular set of educational methods
and he seeks to promote those methods in a chapter
on "Infant Schools." Although published at a time
when James Fenimore Cooper, Thomas Cole, and others
were making the American landscape the subject of a
national literature and art, Scenery and Manners
was primarily the product of another movement: the
effort to establish an American system of education.

Dwight's pedagogical technique consists largely of structuring his reader's experience of the
landscape in such a way as to impress certain
ideas firmly on the mind. This strategy serves two
functions: it demonstrates the methods employed in
the infant schools, which Dwight hoped to see established throughout the nation, and it prepares
American citizens to experience the New England

3

landscape as a textbook of culture. Dwight's book was aimed at families and was designed to help them discover the Christian and republican values he wished to promote in the landscapes they encountered. By teaching people to read the landscape in this religious and patriotic fashion, he hoped to bind the American "social and family circle" more closely to the land.

Theodore Dwight, Jr., a great-grandson of Jonathan Edwards, came naturally to a social vision of the landscape. His father, Theodore Dwight, was a lawyer, newspaper editor, and Connecticut Wit, who spent much of his career in Hartford but later edited newspapers in Albany and New York City. Theodore, Jr., studied with his uncle Timothy at Yale before going on to become an author, editor, and teacher in Manhattan and Brooklyn. His trips to Italy in 1818 and 1820 during a period of revolutionary turmoil profoundly affected his view of the world, and as chapters in Scenery and Manners about travelers from Greece and South America indicate, he remained sympathetic to the struggles of various countries for independence. He later entertained political exiles from the Latin countries of Europe and South America in his home, including Garibaldi. He produced several travel books, including an ordinary guidebook (The Northern Traveller), but none as original as Scenery and Manners. Like his close friend, Lydia H. Sigourney, he helped to nourish the growing cult of domesticity in the 1830s and 1840s. He published a book of advice to fathers on child rearing (The Father's Book, 1834) and edited a family magazine (Dwight's American Magazine and Family Newspaper, 1845-52).

In the late 1820s, when he was writing Scenery and Manners, Dwight's concern with education expressed itself in his support of a movement to establish schools for children between the ages of eighteen months and seven years. The infant schools, as they were called, were originally intended to provide day care for the working poor and to instill morality in their offspring, but Dwight, like other leaders of the movement in the United

4

States, felt that they should serve the children of all classes. Samuel Wilderspin, the British proponent of infant schools, argued that learning should be pleasing, even amusing; that teachers should be cheerful and kind; and that they should nurture the child's curiosity about the world that surrounded him. He believed that if the child's mind were allowed to unfold naturally as God had meant it to, the child would grow into a good person. In Sketches of Scenery and Manners, Dwight extends the infant school idea that children learn naturally from the environment immediately around them to the larger New England region. Travel could play an important role in the American child's development, Dwight felt, if families paid proper attention to the virtues expressed in the American landscape.

Dwight's uncle Timothy was also concerned with the moral values of the American landscape, as were Dwight's contemporaries, James Fenimore Cooper and Thomas Cole, but the most important influences on Theodore Dwight were the ideas about education he borrowed from the Scottish associationists and from English and European thinkers like Samuel Wilderspin and Johann Pestalozzi. He probably became familiar with these ideas in the pages of the influential American Journal of Education where the ferment that led to the establishment of public schools throughout the nation was well under way by 1829.

According to the educational theories Dwight relied on, particularly as they were applied in the infant schools, learning depended heavily on the impact of visual objects on the mind, and that is why travel could readily be turned to educational account. The eye, Dwight wrote later in Things As They Are (1834), is man's "narrow window" on "the vast extent of the Almighty's handiwork." "How diminutive a watchtower is the human frame, how minute is that telescope, yet how wonderful its power. . . ." In Sketches of Scenery and Manners the power of that telescope often discovers the evidence of a republican civilization in the landscape before it. The range of the Ossipee Mountains appears from Red Mountain to be "one great wilderness," for example, but "the eye, on concentrating its power to a needle's point, could here and there distinguish a little spot of brighter green than the common hue of the forests, which, after a moment's attention, would unfold like the germ of an acorn, and show a farm, with its fields, orchard and dwellings." For Dwight such farms reflect the fortitude of their owners, and the effort the eye must make to see the farms imitates the persistence with which the farmers worked the land. "It almost fatigues the eye to follow on from field to field, from farm to farm, from hamlet to village, from town to town," Dwight says in viewing the Connecticut Valley from Mount Holyoke, "what then must have been the amount of labor, the persevering industry, by which the husbandmen of this delightful region have prevailed . . . in covering such a wide extent with one coat of verdure . . .!"

In passages like these, Dwight is less interested in the pictorial values emphasized by earlier writers (like Timothy Dwight in his Travels), than he is in the moral associations the traveler attaches to the scene. In focusing on the thoughts suggested by the landscape, Dwight was no doubt guided by Archibald Alison's Essays on the Nature and Principles of Taste (1790). According to Alison, the spectator's emotional response to the landscape arises from the associations evoked in the mind by objects in the landscape rather than from the physical properties and aesthetic qualities of those objects alone, as Burke had argued. People react most strongly to native places furnished with stories or historical events, Alison argued, because those places bring patriotic ideas to their minds. These Alisonian theories were adopted by American writers in the 1820s. Following the example of Scott, American writers began identifying literary and historical associations in the landscapes they depicted. The incidents of the American Revolution and stories about the American Indian often provided the associations they sought. The experiences of American families also provided

the right material, especially for writers of domestic fiction and sentimental poetry. Dwight
touches only briefly on the American Indian, but he
makes frequent use of the other two motifs in
attempting to educate his readers to the signifi-
cance of their native scenery.

In locating associations with the American
Revolution and the American family in the New England landscape, Dwight employs a symbolic method
that is very much in the Puritan tradition of
typological thinking, but that finds support in the
educational thinking of his contemporaries as well.
W. C. Woodbridge, in a paper entitled "On the Best
Method of Teaching Geography," said that "in order
to employ to the utmost, the power of association,
and to compel the pupil as far as possible to
attach each characteristic of a nation to the spot
on which they reside, I have been led to resort to
the use of emblems." Dwight's use of this pedagogical technique is particularly apparent in the way
in which he makes his entire geography of New
England emblematic of the American Revolution and
the republic it established. French Catholic Canada, which Dwight regards as a backward region
where the progressive forces of civilization are
stultified, marks off the northern boundary. Bennington and Saratoga, where Burgoyne's defeat ended
a threat to New England during the Revolution,
together with the Highlands, where British success
was nullified by Burgoyne's defeat, form the western boundary. The White Mountains represent the
sublime center of this geography both in a natural
and political sense. There the ruins left by the
flooding and avalanching that tore up the Saco
River valley in 1826, fifty years after the Declar-
ation of Independence, become images of the violence of the Revolution, and Dwight uses these
images to imply that if the Revolution was a cataclysmic event, it was also a natural one.

Throughout the book, even small details come
to function as patriotic emblems. The farm that
unfolds "like the germ of an acorn" as the spectator focuses his vision upon the wilderness is

clearly a seed of the American republic, but Dwight
even discovers the oak, as the traditional sign of
the rights of the people, in the view of Lake
Winnepesaukee from Red Mountain. The bays of the
lake look to him like "those lobed oak leaves that
shade the banks, and which the inhabitants weave
into fantastic decorations for their houses."
Dwight condenses the domestic civilization
represented by these homes and farms into his description of individual families, particularly the
family of Samuel Willey, and these descriptions
also serve his educational goals. The Willeys were
by all accounts intelligent, honest, and hospitable
people who kept a small farm in the notch near
Mount Washington and entertained travelers who
passed through that wild opening in the mountains.
When floods and avalanches devastated the region in
1826, one of the slides wiped out the entire family
as they fled from their home. Dwight, like many of
his contemporaries, idealized the Willey family as
the embodiment of Christian and republican values.
While they were alive they had "taught the valley
to repeat the praise of the Almighty," he said.
Their house, which miraculously escaped the devastation, became an emblem of their virtue as well as
a sad reminder of their tragic story and of human
mortality generally. Here was a spot endowed with
the requisite native associations and also an object perfectly adapted to serve as a visual aid in
the moral education of the spectator. An engraving
of the Willey or Notch House appears for precisely
these reasons in Samuel Griswold Goodrich's First
Book of History for Children and Youth (1831),
along with a brief account of the disaster. Goodrich indicates the pedagogical purpose of such
illustrations in the preface to that book: "A large
number of engravings have been inserted as well for
illustrations, as for fixing certain ideas perma-
nently in the memory of the pupil." Like Goodrich,
Dwight tells the story of the Willey Disaster in
order to attach the reader's feelings to an American place, a place that would impress ideas of
virtue upon his mind. Dwight's own engravings also

serve this end. In his effort to instruct the reader in the patriotic and domestic associations of the landscapes he depicts, Dwight also exploits the structure of those landscapes. According to Wilderspin, Pestalozzi, and the other theorists Dwight admired, learning takes place most naturally when it proceeds step by step from what can be apprehended easily with the senses (a flower or a stone) toward the distant or abstract (a star or God). In studying geography, for example, the child would begin with things he could see, like objects on a table, and after learning about how objects are related to each other in space, would move to pictures and maps of what he couldn't see (Italy and Spain, for example). This idea, that ultimately derived from the work of Locke and Rousseau, was a reaction against the mechanical memorization of names and facts that characterized much of education at the time. The method was put into practice in books like Goodrich's The Child's Book of American Geography (1831), in which the child was encouraged to familiarize himself with his surroundings close at hand (his home, classroom, and neighborhood) and work out toward the larger world. Dwight follows the same plan in moving from the familiar landscape of his native Connecticut outward to the more distant features of New England and its bordering regions--Red Mountain in New Hampshire, the White Mountains, Saratoga, lower Canada, and the Hudson Highlands.

On a more metaphysical plane, the assumption, which Dwight would have encountered in Archibald Alison's Essays, that thought ascends by stages from visible objects toward the invisible, also supports this organization of the reader's and traveler's movement through the landscape. As Alison puts it, when the mind takes flight, "we rise from familiar subjects to the sublimest conceptions, and are rapt in the contemplation of whatever is great or beautiful which we see in nature, feel in man, or attribute to the Divinity." In Dwight's account, the entrance to the White Moun-

tains is a perfect diagram of "the constitution of
the human mind" as Alison describes it. The topog-
raphy seems providentially arranged to lead the
mind from the domestic landscape of farms toward
the exalted mountains and the sublime thoughts that
they inspire, from Red Mountain, with its primitive
Indian associations, toward Mount Washington, a
symbol of the highest ideals of civilization. The
landscape that Dwight describes educates the mind
simultaneously to an appreciation of nature and the
American republic. As a "vast avenue" of converging
mountain ranges conducts the traveler "towards the
stupendous White Mountains, he finds the objects
around him well calculated to affect the tone of
his mind, and to prepare him, in some measure, for
what he is hereafter to witness." In the heart of
the White Mountains, Washington, the General and
President, shares the divine associations of the
mountains, while Mount Washington, like similar
"eminences" back in Connecticut, becomes a type of
human greatness: "This is the grand avenue towards
the centre of the White Mountains, where Washington
sits enthroned in the midst of his gigantic associates, usually with a crown of snow upon his
head--the honor conferred by the pure and elevated
regions which he inhabits."
      The position of Dwight's chapter on "Infant
Schools," just after he has described the entrance
to the White Mountains but before his chapter on
the mountains themselves, also reflects his strategy of directing the reader's associations. Why does
Dwight allow this chapter to interrupt his best
descriptive passages? Given his didactic method,
his intention must have been to introduce the con-
cept of the infant school at the point where it was
most likely to gain a foothold in the reader's mind
through its association with the sublimity of the
White Mountains. As he says in Things As They Are,
after reflecting on the image of "hundreds of thousands of children" being instructed simultaneously
all over the country, "Such reflections are impressed upon the mind more deeply by solitude and
agreeable scenery. . . ." In the case of the White

Mountains the scenery had the added advantage of being already laden with American associations and therefore more effective, presumably, in binding the infant school idea into an American framework.

The educational journey that Dwight conducts the reader upon leads finally to the heart of the White Mountains, where the sublimity of the scenery tests the limits of human comprehension. In attempting to deal with the gigantic, Dwight again depends on the educational principles that inform his book. Before the 1826 avalanches he spent his time "in measuring the altitudes above, the magnitudes at any side, and the depths below." In the manner later recommended by Goodrich as a device for teaching geography, he attempted to comprehend the immense objects surrounding him by comparing them to objects which he could grasp more easily: "I tried to form ideas of their dimensions, by imagining some of the most magnificent structures I had ever seen upon their tops; or some of the cities which are visited on account of their grandeur and magnificence, constructed on their sides. . . ." The sight of a tree or a winding stream, or the effects of farmer Willey's scythe, gave relief to "an eye fatigued with measuring rocks, spanning gulfs, and embracing mountains whole, with a labor far disproportioned to its powers or its habits." After the slides had done their work, however, there was nothing to relieve the eye. Now only images of war seemed to offer possible objects for comparison: "There lies a mass of granite, as large as the stone balls thrown by Turkish cannon in the Dardanelles, one of which is sufficient to sink a frigate." In the end, the attempt to associate the ruins left by the cataclysmic events of 1826 with human activities fails to encompass the scene and the spectator is cut loose from the particulars of human history. In the attempt to understand, he is forced to a recognition of the thing itself: "The works of nature alone are seen: every thing is removed which indicates the artificial differences of different countries, and leaves the visitor to feel like a citizen of the world." We have entered,

INTRODUCTION

one might say, a region beyond geography, which
knows neither "the blessings of wise laws," nor
"the oppression of absolute power," and where nature seems to be so pure that she "repels man and
his concerns together."

Dwight guides us through the entire "tour of
education," from the near, visible, and easily
understandable to the universal and difficult to
grasp. Characteristically, however, he takes only a
passing interest in the wild and desolate. For him
the end of education is the nurturing of domestic
civilization, and he therefore concludes his account of the White Mountains by focusing our attention on a family, very much like the Willeys in
their "intellectual refinement" and "religious
feelings," who live on one of the wildest streams
in the region. Timothy Dwight, for whom the village
was the locus of civilization, was disturbed by the
idea of families living on farms beyond the easy
reach of church and school, but Theodore makes them
the very type of social perfection. Their romantic
circumstances enhance their value as models by
providing a memorable context in which their qualities shine forth. The "domestic tranquility and
happiness" of this White Mountain family form "a
strong moral contrast with the unceasing turmoil
and lawless violence which filled the little valley
with loud though inarticulate murmurs." Though
isolated, the family often reads Scott and Shakes-
peare. Dwight attributes this refinement to the
fact that in America knowledge is accessible to
everyone. Whereas "The severe atmosphere and the
sterile soil of a mountainous district, usually
degrade the mind," in our country, "where schools
and books are almost as general and free as the
rain, there are fewer impediments to prevent the
poor from some portion of learning, and not solitary instances of cultivated minds in the most unfavorable situations." Because it is naturally
diffused throughout the land, Dwight implies, education redeems both the American family and the
landscape in which the family is situated.

This metaphor of diffusion or circulation is

the central metaphor of Scenery and Manners. For
Dwight, education and travel are both means of
disseminating moral values. The multitude of farms
in the Connecticut Valley, created out of what was
once a wilderness, make Dwight think of the settlers who have carried their spirit of industry
from Connecticut to colonies in the West; the route
to the White Mountains becomes, as we have seen, an
outline of the progress of knowledge; and Dwight
deplores the fact that the great "current of intelligence" stops at the Canadian border. Dwight ela-
borates further on the metaphor of circulation in
the chapters that follow the section on the White
Mountains. He notes the importance of the veterans
of the Revolution who "cheerfully dispersed to
their homes" after the war and remained as living
emblems of patriotism in a republic. He describes
the travelers to the United States from revolutionary countries who herald the diffusion of "civil,
intellectual and moral light" in their own lands.
And he urges American families to set off as tourists to see the United States.

    J. B. Jackson suggests in "The Necessity of
Ruins" that "it would be easy to relate fashions in
tourist attitudes and objectives to prevailing
educational theories." In Scenery and Manners the
application of educational methods to the formation
of a tourist's response to the landscape was deliberate and specific. The infant school movement,
however, to which the book was tied, flourished in
America for only a brief period, from 1826 until
about 1837. Although the ideas about learning that
the infant schools embodied continued to influence
American education, even the very existence of the
movement was soon forgotten. Dwight's Scenery and
Manners was doomed to a similar obscurity, partly
because Dwight tried to use it as a vehicle to
promote the infant school movement, partly, no
doubt, because tourists found practical guidebooks
like Dwight's Northern Traveller more suited to
their purposes. Nevertheless, Dwight made an original contribution to the New England tradition of
discovering spiritual connections between the peo-

ple of New England and the land which they occu-
pied. <u>Sketches</u> <u>of</u> <u>Scenery</u> <u>and</u> <u>Manners</u> <u>in</u> <u>the</u> <u>United</u>
<u>States</u> survives today as a fascinating attempt to
project the values of a culture into a landscape,
and thereby make the landscape into a school of
citizenship.

JOHN F. SEARS

Vassar College

SKETCHES

OF

SCENERY AND MANNERS

IN THE

UNITED STATES.

BY THE
AUTHOR OF THE "NORTHERN TRAVELLER."

NEW-YORK:

PUBLISHED BY A. T. GOODRICH.

1829.

J. SEYMOUR, PRINTER.

PREFACE.

THE following pages have been composed from materials collected without any original design of publication. The drawings from which the accompanying lithographic prints and etchings have been copied, were also made merely for private gratification. The chief merit of both consists in the excellence of the subjects which they are intended to present to the public, and particularly to the eye of the traveller. In one respect the descriptions and the drawings may be regarded as similar:—they present outlines, generally correct; but the highest embellishments of both must be sought in the originals.

If this volume should excite any new interest in the beauties of our scenery, and in the traits of our manners, those subjects will be found, on further investigation, to be replete with attractions, and to afford inexhaustible themes for agreeable and useful reflection.

INDEX.

LIST OF DRAWINGS.

SKETCHES, &c.

CONNECTICUT RIVER.

In choosing the summit of Mount Holyoke as the spot from which to take a general view of this great stream, I cannot but reflect with pleasure, that it is a favourite spot with travellers, and that the mere mention of its name will excite many agreeable recollections. If there be any thing beautiful in the banks of the Connecticut, those beauties may well be descanted upon here; for in this vicinity are they presented in greater variety, and in a larger extent, than in any other part of its course; and if any eminence may claim particular attention for being extensively known and greatly admired, surely it must be the one on which we have taken our station.

On the banks of the most important stream of New-England, the most delightful, the most populous, the most remarkable in history, this commanding mountain rises, with its steep but woody sides, and overlooks a wide scene of fertility, diversified with the dwellings of an industrious population, and many of those structures which attest the general diffusion of

2

knowledge, refinement, and good habits. He who has visited distant countries, and can recall such scenes as are presented on the banks of the Po, the Arno, and other rivers most celebrated for the richness and high cultivation of their soil, may speak with justice of the inferior extent of the landscape around us, wide spread as it is, and may miss those signs of splendid feudal wealth and power which have never existed in our land. But in every thing which relates to the condition and the character of the inhabitants, he finds room for congratulation and gratitude. He will regard the country which he overlooks as one of the happiest on earth. Here is no corrupt or oppressive system of laws, no arbitrary and vicious ruler, with power to wield a rod of iron. The fertile meadows of the Connecticut, divided into minute parcels by imaginary lines, present a just resemblance to the common rights in which all participate, and the rich intellectual enjoyments which are accessible to every individual. And yet Nature has not, as in so many other regions, exhausted her bounties in bestowing delightful scenes, a benignant climate, and luxuriant crops, to render the intellectual waste more conspicuous : Providence seems rather to have spread before our eyes a display of extraordinary beauty and fertility, the better to lead us to appreciate the blessings he has conferred on the land, in the institutions for government, religion, morality and learning.

If such are the natural reflections of a stranger, what must be those of one who ascends this height with an intimate knowledge of the scene which lies below. To one born on the banks of this river, edu-

cated among its inhabitants, partaking in those attach-
ments to the stream which the natives generally feel for
it in every part of its course ; one nurtured in his
tender years on the rich products of her fields, and
retaining affectionate recollections of early friends
that now rest in its soil—to such an one every point
of view, almost every object to which he can turn,
has something to fix his eye and to engage his thoughts.
The valley below him offers a wide expanse for the
meanderings of the noble river, which pursues its
course in bold and graceful sweeps, bounded, but not
confined, by numerous and conspicuous eminences, that
may remind him of the distinguished families and individuals to which it has at different periods given birth,
with whose virtues or talents he is familiarly acquainted, and whose example he has ever revered. His
memory is stored with the interesting history, and the
varied traditions of this region ; and he reflects atten-
tively on the character and the origin of his forefathers,
the condition of their descendants, and the vast extent to which the world has felt an influence from
them, as well through their example, as by the trans-
planting of their institutions and habits to distant
regions, with the colonies that have departed from
these favourite abodes. Something better than the
vanity of one's country is gratified by this consideration ; for while he attributes to such principles and
institutions the foundation of those traits which in
himself he most approves, philanthropy leads him to
rejoice at their diffusion over the earth, while conscience reminds him how difficult is his task on whom

devolves the duty of supporting a corresponding character.

To him who has duly appreciated and obeyed in
manhood, the precepts of virtue and the upright examples with which he was familiar in youth, scenes
like those of his early life will always be dear; and to
a person of this character, who claims the Connecticut
as his native stream, the country he overlooks from
this position will present an appeal to his heart which
it will be difficult for his lips to describe. Here he
will look down, if not upon the village in which he was
born, upon many a one which in essential points resembles it; and a glance of the eye will suggest to
him the employments and the character of its inhabitants. He knows what race of men dwell in those
farm houses, with what feelings of equality they mingle in the concerns of life, what principles of education are pursued in the schools, as well as what sublime and solemn truths are weekly delivered in the
churches; whither tend the councils of their mothers,
and what the grade of elevation the female character
maintains. The attention will be directed with pleasure to the rustic roads and by-paths which wind their
way towards the secluded and humble dwellings of many
a simple patriarch, in the shady recesses of the hills:
for the spectator knows the characteristics he would
find in active existence among them; and the strong
but now dormant traits, of which he can recall many
an interesting example, when times of public trial
formerly called them into operation; when the Revolution demanded sacrifices—the French and Indian
wars called for courage amidst lamentations—and

when the first settlement of this once inhospitable region introduced our ancestors to the various dangers of unpropitious summers and rigorous winters, and exposed them to wild beasts, and men scarcely less fierce or less savage. By some of those routes did the colonists approach—few, unprotected, and guided only by a hand unseen : by others did their numerous and unrelenting savage enemies wind their cautious and insidious way to attack and destroy them ; or the captives, surprised or overpowered, begin their weary march into exile by the light of their burning houses.

Mount Holyoke presents to the traveller an advantage which it is natural for him to desire : an opportunity to view from an elevated position the most charming scene in the compass of his tour. Fine as the region is, without this eminence half its beauty would have been lost. Or had the position of the mountain been other than it is, there would perhaps have been something to regret. Now, from its lofty and sheltered summit, the visitor overlooks the most fertile and extensive plain the country embraces, with the largest stream in New-England gracefully winding through it, enriching the green surface of the soil with its serpentine band of silver. Richer than the rivers of the south, which rise among mines of gold and silver, the Connecticut dispenses fertility wherever it flows, by means of its periodical floods, and at the same time offers an easy channel of communication to those who dwell upon the banks. In ancient times this stream was first known to our ancestors as that by which the Indians in Canada carried on a trade in skins with those who inhabited the lower parts of its course. Common interests probably promoted peace and amity between the various tribes it visited ; and though circumstances have so greatly changed since that period, the partial navigation to which it is subservient, and still more the constant and easy communication afforded by the level roads along its margin, still tend to unite in fellowship and brotherhood those whom artificial boundaries have nominally divided. The equal favors it distributes on every hand, and even to many of its most remote tributary streams, seem thus to be participated by the people in a moral regard. One description of its natural products has however been heedlessly sacrificed, and the loss is one which must be more and more sensibly felt. These pure waters formerly abounded in fish of the finest species. The salmon of the Connecticut were famous far and wide for their superior flavor, as they had ever been for their abundance. There are many places, particularly at the principal cataracts, where the Indians used annually to assemble to take this valuable prey ; and their broken implements are now to be seen in the soil, in greater numbers than the fish for which they were designed have been found in the river for many a past year. An imperfect, ill executed and unsuccessful plan for the improvement of the navigation, has excluded these invaluable shoals from their favorite stream ; and for the small advantages it was expected to yield, has been allowed to strike a death-blow at a great source of wealth which the river afforded. Could the number of salmon ever caught here in a single season be estimated, and even a distant approximation be made to what might have been

the value of the fishery now, with the present amount
of inhabitants, the people of the Connecticut would
deplore their loss, and be solicitous, at any hazard, to
recover the advantage so unwisely sacrificed. It is
still within the memory of the old, that multitudes of
the finest fish were once caught even in the principal
branches of this river, very far from their confluence:
twenty miles up the Farmington, and thirty miles up
the Ware, the skill of the fisherman was once amply
rewarded. And yet this invaluable bounty of Providence has been yielded up, and is now generally
regarded as irrecoverable. A common belief is, that
the occupations of a great population, particularly in
manufacturing districts, are unfavorable to the habits
or the existence of these timid fish. But they are not
driven from the rivers of Britain, although almost
every obstacle is thrown in their way except that by
which we have succeeded in excluding them : viz. an
actual interruption of the stream so as effectually to
prevent this passage. On the contrary, the supplies in
the Scotch and English rivers appear to be as great as
ever, in spite of the improper and illegal fishing
which is carried on, together with the destruction of
millions of young every year. Of the value of those
fisheries, perhaps it is impossible to form a precise
idea ; but it is well known that thousands of pounds
are the annual incomes of the right to fish within the
limits of certain single estates. The oversight of our
countrymen is however inexcusable, in not adopting
some simple means to render the dams in the Connecticut and its branches passable by these fine fish.
With their remarkable activity the highest falls were

readily ascended by them every season; and doubtless a sufficient current of water, allowed to run even
a part of the time, as during the night, might have
afforded them access to all parts of the stream. Some
of the small fish which afford a considerable addition
to the stock of food along the coast of Massachusetts
Bay, are thus allowed to visit the ponds and head
streams of brooks, which would otherwise be closed
against them by the dams; and a similar experiment
might perhaps prove successful here. Instead of the
works on the stream being rendered less valuable by
the small expense and the little loss of water that
might be required to keep open the passage, the
restoration of their shoals to the river and its branches,
if it could be effected by such means, would produce
a large accession to the number of inhabitants, and
greatly increase the amount of exports and imports
throughout the extensive valley of the Connecticut.

The space on the summit of Mount Holyoke is so
small, that, from the building on the peak, where the
visiter will find shelter and refreshment, the eye ranges
without interruption in every direction. The accompanying print may afford a feeble idea of the finest part
of the scene, which stretches northward along the
wide and fertile meadows that border the Connecticut,
and affords it a more spacious range for its meanderings than in any other part of its course. It would be
an almost hopeless task for an artist, to attempt the
representation of all the beauties which are here presented in one view to the eye. Small as is the point
of the pencil, and delicate as is the touch of the graver,
even when directed under the magnifier, they are still

View of Connecticut River.

from Mount Hanyto

too broad to depict without blending the countless
lines, which denote the thousands of little fields that
cover the surface with a rich party-colored hue.   The
assiduous artist, seating himself on one of these rocks,
to transfer the scene to his sketch book, would sigh
in despair at the amount of labor required to detail all
the minute divisions and features which so thickly
overspread even a small portion of the country.   It
almost fatigues the eye to follow on from field to field,
from farm to farm, from hamlet to village, from town
to town;—what then must have been the amount of
labor, the persevering industry, by which the husbandmen of this delightful region have prevailed, by individual exertions and slow degrees, in covering such a
wide extent with one coat of verdure : casting into the
ground every seed from which the green pastures and
the waving wheat fields have sprung, and planting
and cherishing every blade which helps to compose
the ten thousand patches of corn !   The institutions
under which these people are born and bred, have
not been in operation for so many years without
stamping their seal on the character and manners of
society ; and so deep is the impression generally produced, that something of the same spirit has been
borne with their colonies, to the western regions they
have gone to occupy.   Churches and school-houses,
good roads and good bridges, have intimated to many
a traveller in our western districts, his vicinity to their
settlements ; and if he has been reared in the same
scenes with them, he will recognise the fruit of their
engrafted orchards, observe well-known customs in
their houses, hear good old maxims in the conversa-

tion of their elders, and find firm moral sentiments existing among all classes, together with a dutiful and reverential attachment to the country of their origin, which they assiduously endeavor to transmit to their posterity.

The inhabitants of the country bordering on the Connecticut, during the first century and a half after its settlement, were deeply engaged in the various contests which were carried on at different periods and with different enemies. The earliest colonists, who took up their station at Hartford, Windsor and Wethersfield, mustered as soldiers a few months after their arrival, and almost exterminated a powerful tribe of Indians, by whom their existence was threatened. After a period of twenty years of peace, Philip's war ravaged the settlements along this stream, which then extended to Northfield, some of which were deserted, some burnt; and sprinkled the shores with blood, often barbarously shed. In the French wars such scenes were renewed in the upper settlements, some of which are included in the region beneath our eyes; and the more distant and serious battles to which they gave occasion were shared, to a large extent, and many of them were influenced or decided, by the inhabitants of this delightful country. In the war of the Revolution, the people of this district performed too conspicuous a part to require particular mention; although, fortunately for the people, it never became the scene of foreign aggression.

There is a remark often repeated concerning the Connecticut, and that with an honest pride, that it

has never been crossed by a foreign foe. Considering the length of its course, the rich and important
districts through which it runs, the great military
events which have occurred on different sides, the
deep concern the people have taken in various wars,
this must be regarded as a remarkable fact. No
enemy of more importance than those who composed
the savage expeditions directed against the frontiers
in early times, had ever crossed the stream; and no
hostile foot has since trodden the soil, if we except the
landing of a marauding party at a little village near
its mouth during the late war with Great Britain.
This has not been for the want of enemies. The
battle of Bunker's hill contributed to keep the English
shut up in the neighbourhood of Boston; and some
of the officers and soldiers engaged in it fought for
the security of homes which were beneath the shadow of these mountains. The check given to Burgoyne's detachment at Bennington placed it out of his
power to move further eastward; and the militia from
this stream assisted on that occasion. The Connecticut is indeed less exposed to the attempts of invaders
than the Hudson, as that river is navigable to a greater
distance, and forms part of the great chain of communication between the Atlantic and the St. Lawrence.
Still, although it seems placed by nature with many
advantages for peace, it has never been wanting in
the resources or the men for self-defence.

The first inhabitants, who might have still possessed
their country, but for that race who were destined
soon to overspread the soil, and eradicate every
trace of its original occupants, are now gone. We

look in vain on the rocks around us for any testimony
of their existence : not an inscription, not a mark is
any where to be found ; and we may scrutinize with
our utmost care the whole region below us, without
discovering a single monument to their virtues or their
misfortunes. A few rude implements or broken weapons of war, with a few traditionary tales, as scattered
and as rare, are all that now remains of the original
possessors of the soil—the people who first knew the
beauties of this river and its meadows, and who shed
their blood in vain to preserve them.

The villages beneath our eyes mark the sites of
ancient Indian towns, whose inhabitants long entertained the white men as friends, and allowed them to
construct their houses among them. When however
the latter grew strong, they made the Indians confine themselves to spots in their vicinity, and surrounded their dwellings with defences. Philip's war, which
suddenly burst out in 1675, extended to nearly all the
Indians throughout the country, and gave rise to
repeated disasters here. This plain was crossed and
recrossed by different hostile parties, thirsty for blood,
and not unfrequently gratified to the full. The scene
has been illuminated at night by the flames of many a
quiet and peaceful dwelling: for all the old villages
were repeatedly attacked, and partly, if not wholly
destroyed by fire. Savage warriors have no doubt
stood on this eminence as on a watch tower, and observed the motions of friend or foe; and once, as tradition informs us, an unfortunate woman, who had
been surprised and taken captive from the hamlet
between the two mountains, was led up and toma-

hawked in the cruel manner of the savages. The plots laid for the extermination of the whites were however unsuccessful, although devised by the sagacity of Philip; and the ambushes, the surprises, the resistance and the endurance of the red men finally proved to be vain, although sometimes partially successful.

Civilization lent arts and power which the uncultured savages could not withstand; and during the peace which succeeded the downfall of Philip, the frontiers were pressed onwards beyond the hills, which bound our northern view. The wars introduced by the bitterness of the French from Canada, did indeed sometimes extend terror, and even bloodshed, to these otherwise peaceful scenes; and there are now to be seen among the collections of ancient records some of those little manuscripts then occasionally borne by friendly Indian messengers from settlement to settlement, announcing dangers which filled every breast with apprehension.

This is a brief outline of the subjects which render this place so deservedly interesting.

Tales of interest might be told of almost every hill, plain, and brook within the bounds of the extensive and fertile valley of the Connecticut. There is an eminence, many miles south of this mountain, of little importance when viewed from a distance, but which is of laborious ascent when actually encountered by the traveller, and delightful and commanding in its

3

view when its summit is once attained. Sloping to
the north it overlooks a portion of the innumerable
level fields of this extensive valley, with that part
of the river's course, which indicates to the anti-
quary's eye the limit of the journey of the first white
men who ever kindled a fire on its banks; and
a broad and beautiful cove, which was the scene of
their trials during the wintry season. Villages now
vary the scenes where the dark forest was once diversified only by the few encroachments of a savage
race; and among all the dwellings (of which each
bears its history) none is more reverend or more delightfully situated, than that of which we are to speak,
whose memory is dedicated by filial affection and
duty. Eighty or one hundred years ago, a more
lowly dwelling, at a little distance, reared its moss-
covered roof. Lessons of religion had blessed it, and
long but humble lives of piety in its two reverend inhabitants, had rendered it sacred. He who had been
the object of their love and prayers had long been
gone; and like many of the wandering sons of New-
England, seemed forgotten by all but the parental
heart. There was one above, however, who still
watched over and protected him. One evening a
stranger came slowly up the hill, and looked with more
than common interest on the scene around him.—
He moved towards the humble dwelling, and was
received with welcome cordiality at a fireside which
few had sought, and from which none had ever been
repelled. The spirit of hospitality displayed itself:
the stranger was welcomed, and no curious question
was applied to unriddle what they thought mysterious.

" Wherever you have travelled over the surface of the
earth," said the mother, "you may perhaps have seen
our son—once our darling boy—do you remember him,
a stranger, a wanderer, a misguided youth, but generous
and kind? He must have spoken with sorrow of his
native land ; he must have talked with tears of his
home and his parents. Perhaps you may have passed
where he lay, for I have often looked upon him as
dead, and my dreams have told me it was true—perhaps you may have seen his grave. Even then it
would be some consolation to hear you speak of it—
for when a babe, he rested on this breast."

The tears which the old parents poured anew as they
thus recurred to their long-lost child, made the stranger
almost regret that he had given rise to a new flood of
grief, which time had done so much to dry up. Nor
did he delay to offer them consolation. The old
matron with surprise saw him turn away with tears
and sobs, and heard him exclaim—" Oh, my mother !
I am your son !"

The scene occurred unwitnessed by others, and
only the outlines of the tale have come down to us.—
The already knotted trunks of the apple trees in an
orchard which partly shades the road, are older than
those which shaded the grass plot before that humble
door, although one of their intermediate generations has flourished and decayed. Yonder mansion.
embosomed in tall and spreading elms, with all its
patriarchal dignity, began to rise the same year in
which this dutiful son was restored to his parents ; and
there they spent in happiness the evening hours
of their day, so much of which had passed in sorrow.

This old and simple story has been narrated here, because the deed it records has in some of our eyes conferred a dignity on the place, of a different but no less affecting nature than it might have derived from those works of art, or monuments to past greatness, which are the boast of many famous scenes.

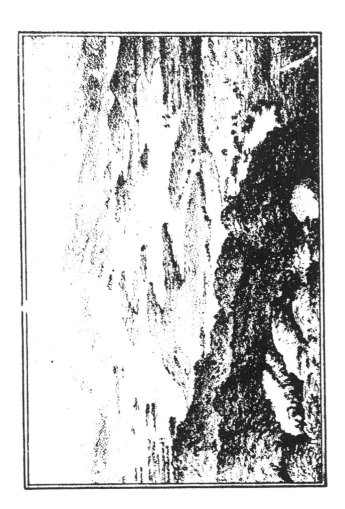

Winnipiseogee Lake

from Red Mountain

RED MOUNTAIN,

IN NEW HAMPSHIRE.

As the traveller seats himself, almost breathless, on the uppermost rock of Red Mountain, he may congratulate himself that he has reached an eminence properly regarded as one of the most enviable, as well as difficult of access, in the circuit of his tour.   I had been fortunate in reaching it, as I had designed, at an early hour in the morning, a short time after the sun had risen ; and found the air fresh and clear, and the surrounding scene delightfully varied by the slanting light.

On the West the eye descended, by giant's strides, down the mountain's side, from rock to tree, from tree to grove, and glanced over the shaded forest that skirted the base, and extended to the shore of a gleaming sheet of water, which lay surrounded on several sides by hills of nearly equal height with that on which I stood.   This was Squam Lake, which lies at the bottom of a great goblet, several miles in circumference. Its shores are mountainous and steep, occupied by a scattered population, animated by a few farms, and marked here and there by a stony road, whose frequent windings indicate the laborious ascents it has to surmount.

3*

Eastward lay a heavy mass of shade, like a black cloud overspreading all that portion of the horizon; and this, on investigation, proved to be the enor. mous bulk of Ossipee Mountains. All that range appeared at first view to be one great wilderness; but the eye, on concentrating its power to a needle's point, could here and there distinguish a little spot of brighter green than the common hue of the forests, which, after a moment's attention, would unfold like the germ of an acorn, and show a farm, with its fields, orchard and dwellings; and as the sun gradually rose higher and rendered distant objects more distinct, such spots became very numerous, so that the lower regions of that lofty range, proved to be well peopled and well cultivated.

Northward, two ranges of lofty summits extended far onward, in parallel directions. Those on the left were shining in the light of morning; while those on the right were half concealed by the mists of the night, then fast leaving the valley. The sun had visited the little lakes and streams which lay in the broad valley between, and some of them were betrayed from afar by bright gleams of light. This is the grand avenue towards the centre of the White Mountains, where Washington sits enthroned in the midst of his gigantic associates, usually with a crown of snow upon his head—the honor conferred by the pure and elevated regions which he inhabits. Through this ample passage may have flowed, in some unrecorded age, one of those mighty currents of water, the traces of which are observed in different parts of our country, as well as in foreign lands. We may at least fancy we trace its course with our eye, as it seems imperfectly indicated by the little sheets of water, left, as it were, in the lower parts of its channel. On closer investigation also, we may observe an immense quantity of granite rocks, which are strewed over the surface for many miles both above and below. Those separate masses, which the present generation are quarrying, with such avidity and advantage, all along the Merrimac river, and which have furnished materials for the construction of edifices in the principal cities in the United States, afford but a feeble idea of the supplies that might be obtained between this place and the White Mountains, from which some almost inconceivable convulsion appears to have dissevered rocks enough to overspread several hundred square miles; while the same or some other power has been able to bear them to the places where we find them at the present day. This power we commonly refer to currents of water, such as may have been produced in the universal deluge, by the breaking up of the fountains of the " Great Deep"; and the further our observations are extended, the more is this conjecture confirmed. It is an irresistible conclusion to which we are led, that the rocks in question have been thus torn from some vast quarry of granite : for they are seen lying over the surface, or near it, on the different soils and rocks which are found between the White Mountains and the neighbouring parts of the Atlantic coast ; and even a hasty observer will trace a resemblance in their color, texture, and various aspects, with those which impede his path, or threaten to fall upon his head, in the narrow passes through which the upper part of the road will conduct him.

Beneath our feet the stones of Red Mountain are crumbling, under the action of the elements. In this they differ from most of the rocks we observe in the lower districts of the state. They differ also in their reddish brown color, on account of which they dispute with the whortleberry bushes (of nearly the same hue in Autumn) the honor of conferring a name on this eminence, so favored in the beauty of its situation. Other varieties of granite may perhaps be found in the vicinity of the mountains, which have gradually dis-integrated when broken and scattered in the open air. A bed of fine white clay was discovered five or six years ago, on the eastern shore of Winnipiseogee Lake, resembling, at least in external characters, some of the porcelain clays of Europe, which are known to have been produced by the decay of that variety of primitive rocks called Graphic Granite.

In a notice of the loose rocks found along the coast of New Hampshire, which was published two or three years since in that valuable work, the American Jour-nal of Science and the Arts, a curious fact was men-tioned. The writer stated, that those boulders had been generally observed to bear grooves on their lower sides, as if they had been forcibly drawn or driven over a rough surface ; while the upper faces of those various rocky beds that are in some places uncovered, present marks of a similar description, running in the general direction in which the boulders are supposed to have passed, and without regard to the courses of the natural strata.

It was up the great valley before spoken of as open-ing northward, that the bold but unfortunate band passed who assailed a nation of Indians, the terror of the frontier below, in the year 1725, under Captain Lovel ; and some of the survivors suffered extreme distress, in regaining, by the same route, the habitations of civilized men after their bloody defeat. That region, so abounding in mountains and small lakes, although in its present, half-tamed condition, so uninviting to man, was the theatre of more than one hostile incursion, in that early period when it was inhabited only by wild beasts and savages ; and some scattering traditions are still to be found, which awaken an interest in the traveller. Doubtless there have been many unrecorded tales of still anterior date, which we might listen to with attention ; for the passes of the White Mountains had been known and visited by the Indians from time immemorial. But we look in vain for any unquestionable monuments to their once powerful tribes, though the singular situation of some of the mighty rocks balanced on the hills, the apparently artificial heaps of loose stones here and there, and the unaccountable lines and figures traced on many rude blocks of granite, in which we are apt to fancy a resemblance to animals, men, or warlike weapons, frequently lead us to think of those wild huntsmen, whose steps have failed in these forests for ever.

But it is almost unpardonable to have so long delayed the notice of that part of the scene which lies south of us, and which was not first described, because its superior beauty would have perhaps diminished the interest of the rest of this extensive landscape. Turning in that direction, the spectator on this commanding eminence finds his eye embracing with delight one of

the most beautiful sheets of water that our country has
to offer among all its varieties. In passing along its
shores he has probably, ere this, been attracted by the
constant but never-wearying succession of headlands
and islands, and been amused by endeavoring to thread
out the labyrinths of the numerous channels which
separate them. Here he first perceives the whole
extent of the lake, and ascertains that he might in vain
have attempted to guide his doubtful way among the
intricacy of passages far more numerous, and leading
to much greater distances than he could have supposed.

The accompanying print may afford some idea of
the scene, although it comprehends only a limited
space, as it was copied from a drawing made from the
spot on which we suppose ourselves to be standing, and
presents, with general accuracy, its prevailing characteristics : undulated shores, long promontories, often
ramified into points, intermingled with islands and
rocks, coves, channels and bays, whose little recesses
have suggested a comparison to the form of those lobed
oak leaves that shade the banks, and which the inhabitants weave into fantastic decorations for their houses.
The islands, although none of them have much elevation, present a great variety of form and size. Cultivation has as yet but feebly impressed its stamp upon
the scene. The fields which skirt several of the
neighbouring villages, are distinguishable at considerable intervals ; and the lower regions of the Ossipee
range, as well as most of the eastern shore of the
lake, appear like a well peopled country. Several of
the larger islands also exhibit farms and hamlets, with
capacious barns and comfortable dwellings ; but their

inhabitants, who amount to but a small number in all, are in a great degree cut off from intercourse with the neighbouring shores, and deprived of many of those advantages which are generally enjoyed in larger communities in this part of the Union. Both churches and school houses are wanting; and the useful information continually traversing the country by innumerable routes, does not easily find its way to them.

A ride along the banks of this beautiful lake, and still more an excursion by water among the labyrinths of the islands and promontories, will afford a great variety of agreeable points of view to the admirer of such scenery; while the numerous fish which are ever eager for the bait, and the water-fowl and forest game to be found in their seasons, offer sufficient amusement for the sportsman. Perch are the fish which chiefly abound; but there are also many trout. The latter are principally taken in the winter, to be sent to the Boston market. The adjoining lake, though of much inferior extent, affords these fine fish of far superior size, and in greater abundance; and the number killed with spears under the ice is often very great.

As the traveller leaves this attractive vicinity and pursues his way up the valley, which conducts him, like a vast avenue, towards the stupendous White Mountains, he finds the objects around him well calculated to affect the tone of his mind, and to prepare him, in some measure, for what he is hereafter to witness. He now perceives that he is gradually leaving the habitations of men, which he finds scattered among the extensive solitudes with a sparing hand.

He is pursuing the path which, from the summit of Red Mountain can barely be distinguished, like a spider's web, stretching along the margin of the valley. Here and there is a hamlet, and at much rarer intervals, a church or two appear, with a few openings in the forest between them; while the fine swelling uplands, being more exposed to view, sometimes present a succession of extensive farms, overspreading a bold and beautiful slope. Partly up these elevations, and partly round their bases, the road proceeds in a winding course; and thus a constantly varying scene is presented, of swelling hills, level little meadows and narrow ravines; uplands half divested of their forests, with the lofty peaks rising above, some with granite foreheads, bared like the bald eagle's, others wooded to their summits, or wearing a single seal of cultivation in a solitary clearing: all these are by turns shut out and revealed by the skirts of the forest mantle, which is so ample in its folds, and diversified in its hues and aspects by the shades and lights of morning and evening, and the effects of mists, clouds, and storms.

It is proverbial of the inhabitants of mountainous regions, that they are inclined to superstition. In travelling up the great avenue from Winnipiseogee Lake to the White Hills, some indications of a popular love for the supernatural may be observed. There is a fine elevation among the range bordering this valley on the left, which is conspicuous for the richness and verdure of the sloping ground that rises far up from its base. The eye is attracted by the natural form of the land, so well calculated for convenient culture, and by the unusual number and extent of the pasture grounds by which it is overspread. A solitary traveller feels tempted from the beaten but almost uninhabited road, to seek society among the people who have so successfully diffused an aspect of civilization over that favored region ; and inquires of the first person he meets, something concerning their condition.

The keeper of a small inn, a few miles north of this place, once communicated the following tradition to a stranger who had taken lodgings at his house, and who, while watching the clearing away of a thunder shower, admired the appearance of the mountain, and particularly the beautiful cultivated land on its sides and base. " The mountain," said he, "is said to owe its name to an old Indian, called Chocaway, who lived by himself in a little wigwam, near a fine spring of pure water, which divides into several branches, and gives the land this green appearance even in the driest seasons of the year. He was known to many white men, although the settlements about Dover were at that time the nearest points where civilized men had dared to fix any permanent habitation. Hunters were not unfrequently found among the hardy settlers, who ranged these extensive forests for deer, bears and buffalo ; and in times of danger, scouting and scalping parties were sent out to discover, and if possible to prevent the approach of French and Indian invaders, by whom the feeble colonies were more than once attacked and laid waste. Although living near the

4

route so frequently pursued by friends and foes, old
Chocaway took no part in the strife, and even appears
to have abstained from shedding the blood even of
brutes, as he spent a solitary and reflecting life in cul-
tivating a little corn, a few beans and squashes, and in
administering to the aid and comfort of those who lost
their way in the chase, or had suffered from want or
wounds in war. For this character he was extensively known, and generally regarded with merited respect.
The infirmities of age had already assailed him, but
he bore his trials and his solitude with such contentment, that he was by some thought to enjoy a melancholy pleasure in the daily contemplation of long-past
scenes of fond affection; while the greater part
believed him in correspondence with some supernatural spirit, which administered to his earthly wants,
and gave him more than earthly knowledge and
power.

One day his retired and silent retreat was intruded
upon by a party of white men accoutred like half-
hunters, half-murderers. They approached him with
none of that reverence which had been so long spontaneously rendered to him by the civilized man and the
savage, and their manners were rude and harsh to one
who had so often kindly entreated such as they, and
perhaps had brought a refreshing draught, or culled
healing herbs, for some individuals of their number.
Their weapons of death were displayed in his presence, but his heart seemed neither to be hastened
nor chilled in its motion. They thundered out, in a
few words in his language—"Old man, you must die!"
but his countenance was as calm and benignant as

ever. The government of the Massachussets had
despatched this party of cold blooded man-hunters,
with a large promise for every Indian scalp they should
take, and here they had sought their first and easiest
prey. But a moment was allowed the old hermit for
a prayer to the Great Spirit, which he chanted in a
few solemn words over the head fountain of those
waters which pour down the mountain's side. The
curses which he denounced on men who, by such
means, were getting possession of the land of his
ancestors, were delivered in so deep and deliberate a
tone, that they made his persecutors shudder, and
nothing but gold could have urged them to accomplish
their purpose. The form of the old man was soon
stretched beside his favorite fountain; and the few
drops of blood which age had left in his cold veins,
were mingled with its waters and borne over the acres
of rich fields which lie so delightfully exposed to the
sun, bearing along a curse which has ever since been
inherent to the soil. That curse the popular voice
declares was designed by him to have a figurative
fulfilment: but by the kindness of Providence has only
been verified according to the letter. He prayed the
Great Spirit that no animal that parted the hoof
might ever live on the mountain's side, believing that
white men could not subsist without assistance from
the labor of the ox; and it is an unquestionable fact,
and one to which I am a witness, that the finest cattle
begin to lose their vigor on being pastured on that
ground, and if kept there a few weeks, pine away
and die without any assignable cause, and in spite
of every precaution and remedy.

INFANT SCHOOLS.

In the institutions recently opened in New-York, Philadelphia, Boston, and many of our inferior cities and towns, for the systematic instruction of very young children, called Infant Schools, travellers of intelligence and rational curiosity will find prepared for them new subjects of attention and interest. The system on which they are formed, was never introduced into the United States until the year 1827, although it had been in operation in Great Britain for several years : probably because no full and methodical account, as is said, has ever been laid before the world. It is of such a boundless nature that continual variations and improvements are necessarily introduced ; and those who become the greatest proficients in teaching according to its principles, are generally too much occupied in their labors, or too much engaged in pursuing their various modes and improvements, to have leisure for drawing up a regular and complete plan of the whole. Numerous books relating to the subject have been published ; and those who are desirous of learning the outlines of the system, or such as may be able to promote the establishment of infant schools in their own distant towns or villages, will obtain a useful supply of different publications of the kind, some containing hints to instructors, and others the exercises of pupils, at the children's book-stores in New-York, and probably in other cities.

Infant schools are peculiarly applicable to large places, where great numbers of poor parents, by being relieved from the care and oversight of their little children for most of the day, are able to apply themselves to occupations, in which they can earn enough to defray the trivial, and often merely nominal expense at which the instruction is afforded, and at the same time add to the comfort of their families. More than twenty Infant Schools are known to be in operation in this country; and probably a considerably greater number might be ascertained. Many of these are designed for the instruction of the children of parents in the middle and upper walks of life; and schools of both descriptions will, it is to be hoped, ere long, be universally known. To promote their general adoption it is that a chapter is here devoted to the subject.

Many persons of experience in the character and capacities of young children, will find one visit to an infant school enough to convince them, that the system may be advantageously introduced into country villages, and even into small neighborhoods or hamlets. Persons of intelligence and of wealth are by no means wanting, in some of the most refined of our country towns, who have already been desirous of resorting to this system for the benefit of their own children. In truth there is much reason for parents in the higher circles of society to apprehend, that unless they follow such an example, or introduce the principles of Infant Schools into their nurseries, their children will be inferior to those of their poor neighbors, in early education. The object of the following remarks is to direct the attention of influential travellers to the Infant Schools, and to induce those who are interested to examine whether the principles of this method of instruction, cannot be in some manner, and to some degree, if not introduced, at least engrafted, on the plan they have adopted at home in their schools or their families.

An objection will occur to the minds of many, on entering a school of this kind in one of our large cities, against the mingling of children of different classes. And this is certainly an obvious and well-founded objection. In great cities there is and must be a difference of manners prevailing among different ranks: and whatever ideas ultra-republicans may entertain, it would do only harm to place the children of poor and rich side by side, to make the former ashamed, and the latter vain of clothes which are really appropriate to their respective spheres, and to excite ill-founded feelings between them at an age when they cannot reason soundly on the subject.—Where greater equality exists, as in many of our villages, no objection of the kind ought to be made; and if, in any case, doubt or fastidiousness should be felt, those who view the matter aright, will be disposed to yield to the important interests of their children.

As an hour spent in witnessing the operation of an Infant School will better instruct a stranger in the principles on which they are conducted, than pages

of description, only a few words will be here said on
the subject.   The whole system may be said to hinge
on the most obvious and simple doctrines :—that chil.
dren of very tender age are capable of being taught
something ; but that in order to convey to their minds
knowledge which they can comprehend, modes must
be adopted calculated also for their intellects.   Sub.
jects which cannot be comprehended by the pupils,
are therefore rejected, and the mind is led to the ac.
quisition of what is within the scope of its capacities,
by the easiest and most direct routes.   It is led like
an intelligent being through gradations of known ideas :
not driven like a brute, with whip and spur, over the
mere emblems and implements of learning.   In this
we follow the system of nature, and we reduce the
plan of infantile instruction to the rules which govern
every other species.   Hitherto children have been
taught the rudiments of knowledge in a way which
would have discouraged a mature mind.   There are
still many advocates for pursuing the ancient system,
prejudiced by immemorial and universal usage : but
if those learned men who support it would reflect how,
if presented to them in that form, all the beauties of
science and literature would be changed to deformity,
and how they would close their libraries in disgust and
extinguish their night lamps, they could not fail to be
convinced of their error.

Why should we counteract the course of nature in
our earliest discipline of the infant mind, and lay the
most disheartening obstacles in the way of an opening
intellect, whose only exertions are voluntary, which is
capable of proceeding, under proper direction, from

the first simple perceptions of light and warmth, pleasure and pain, to comprehend the fullest scope of the
sciences, to embrace the world in its grasp, to encompass the firmament, and to adore and imitate the character of the Almighty ?

In the usual systems of instruction, the child finds
himself subjected to a mode the opposite of that
which he has experienced before his introduction to
school. Then he found a world full of novelties
around him, such as were understood by others, and
which he felt a constant desire to understand. The
nature, and the uses of many objects he was able to
ascertain before he could call their names, by
giving attention to them one by one ; and of others he
received much more information when he became able
to inquire of his parents, and to comprehend their
explanations. Wherever he went, whatever he did,
he was at school, but at school to Dame Nature ; and
his progress and his prospects were of a flattering
description. But see the change, when transferred
from her kind and simple teaching, to the artificial
process of a misled instructor of human mould. The
uncomfortable situation in which he is placed at his
elevated form, with no rest for his feet and no support
for his back, at a height from the floor terrific to his
infantile eyes, forms but an imperfect type of the unnecessary, painful, and injurious constraints to which
his mind is subjected.

Those who regard the treatment of young children
at school in this light, may well lament the errors of
the system under which so many generations have
been tortured rather than instructed, and wish that it

might be universally substituted throughout the world by one of a more humane, rational, and effectual character.

When a child has once entered a school, he finds that what he is thenceforward to learn is to be obtained in a way entirely new, and which he cannot comprehend. The acquisition of knowledge is from that moment stripped of all its attractions. In vain he inquires why or how things are so. These spontaneous questions, which he formerly uttered with eager curiosity, while he listened to the answers with satisfaction and delight, he is no longer permitted to use.— Mystical forms are presented to him, over which he is required to pronounce words unmeaning to his ears, and with which his mind learns to associate nothing but frowns and blows. The memory is wearied with a mass of chaotic sounds and figures, in which he can find neither correspondence nor use; the intellect sickens, because it is treated with contempt as well as neglect; and this system, although it somewhat relents in its severity in subsequent years, greatly prevails through the whole tour of education, and forms a powerful barrier to his progress at every stage. It probably will appear clear to every observing mind, that many a child possessed of capacity and a disposition to acquire knowledge, has received a shock on undergoing this translation from the system of nature to that of art, from which it has never recovered. It has fallen under the observation of every one, that many of the most backward and dilatory scholars are the most active and ingenious at their sports. In many cases they are found to excel as much out of school

in those things which require a critical observation
and laborious mental exertion, as in mere feats of
athletic superiority. The reason may be, that every
thing which they find without the walls of the school-
house, they are permitted to investigate, and to become
acquainted with in the direct and simple way.

And thus it has so often happened, that the young
have made much more rapid progress in evil than in
good, because the acquisition of what is useful is im-
peded by artificial and unnecessary restraints, from
which the knowledge of evil is entirely free and unshackled.

These restraints, these shackles, are various and innumerable. Among them should be ranked every
unintelligible word, and every process that keeps the
mind in unnecessary suspense. Our most intelligent
and experienced teachers will readily admit, that one
leading defect of the common modes of instruction consists in teaching words which are not connected with
their appropriate ideas in the minds of the children.
It is in vain for the young lips to be able to repeat
such words; for the utmost that such an acquisition
can effect, is to impose upon some of those who hear
them, and to make others doubly sensible of their deficiencies in real knowledge. The ideas should be
first implanted, and then the words will be ready on
the lips, without the labor of acquiring them by frequent
repetitions. The vicious system here condemned is
fit for nothing but parrots or learned brutes; and cannot be applied to the human mind without a grave and
practical contempt for its nature, and setting at nought
its powers. All branches of instruction will be found

to be more or less conducted on such principles in this country. We meet with different ramifications of this vicious system in our families, our primary schools, and those of the higher grades, up to our gymnasia and colleges. Individuals have perhaps ever opposed it, to such extent as they were able, in institutions of different kinds ; but the public prejudices, as well as the books, being generally formed on the erroneous principles, they have found great difficulties in teaching as they would wish, and still greater in bringing about any extensive change. Towards it, however, we have to hope for a powerful co-operation among our literary individuals and literary institutions ; and now that a reformation has been introduced at the root of education, in the plans adopted in Infant Schools, there is great reason to look for its effect on the whole, even to the trunk and branches. In that case, of course, we may expect early blossoms and fruit of an improved description.

It may be questioned, whether the study of grammar has not been thus far subjected to the most grievous burthen of unintelligible words and phrases ; and perhaps we should naturally imagine it the most difficult branch of youthful instruction to be divested of them, so as to be presented in a comprehensible form. At the Infant School in Greene street, New-York, which is the model school of that city, a simplified system of grammar has been introduced, which is built on fundamental improvement, although still open to such alterations as intelligent minds might suggest, and the curious feel disposed to test by experiment.

Of all the subjects that could have been selected in a book like this little volume, none could be expected to find in that class which every author should be most ambitious to gratify, so large a number of attentive readers and capable judges. Every parent has some acquaintance with the subject, and that kind of acquaintance which ensures a feeling of strong interest. The importance of it has been pressed home on the parental bosom by the tender love of children; the imperfection of the systems and doctrines in vogue have been realized from personal trial and ill success; the want of a thorough reformation in every part has been ascertained by convincing experience; the difficulty of accomplishing appears almost insuperable, after repeated vain attempts to improve; while the further the subject has been studied, the more extensive and complicated has it appeared, the more worthy of investigation, the more culpably neglected. Many persons in such a state of mind, have cast a glance at an Infant School, and exclaimed that all is now done. Parents, more naturally than others, are led to turn their thoughts to consider the influence of education; but those who begin by tracing its effects on their own minds, their own lives and their own prospects, and then extend their view to the community in which they live, to their country and the world, can easily satisfy themselves that it is of vast consequence and universal concern.

So powerful is its operation on individuals and countries, that to make a mutual transfer of the systems of education practised in two different and distant countries, would be, in fact, in a short course of

5

time, a virtual exchange of inhabitants. On a small scale this fact is every day acknowledged, because it is every day proved. Education is the chief human means by which individuals and families are daily rising on one side of us and falling on the other. By education is not meant merely the instruction in letters which a school-master or a professor can communicate, or pretends to communicate; and every judge of the subject, every parent, will uphold the justice of taking a more extended view. Education includes every branch and kind of information communicated to the youthful mind by design—it also includes all communicated by permission. Here then, on this broad scale, we include every thing that comes to the youthful mind with a force likely to exercise an influence; and the channels through which it may approach: even the language of deeds and of looks, as well as of words. Example will be included as well as precept. Education very naturally divides itself into two species—moral and intellectual, yet the two are so dependant on each other, that they cannot be safely separated. It would be very dangerous, for example, to trust to a bad man the instruction of a child in any branch of knowledge, however superior might be his acquaintance with it. It is also injudicious to make a remarkably ignorant man display his ignorance to a child he might be able to lead in all good moral and religious ways, both by precept and example. Not only so, but the various moral qualities and habits which are necessary to the pupil, in whatever branch of learning he may be progressing, should if possible be exhibited in the conduct of the teacher. A child will not dis-

'criminate between what he sees and hears, and what he is directed to see and hear. A teacher may be paid for instructing in arithmetic, music, or a language; but he exhibits feelings, he expresses opinions, he betrays partialities or antipathies on many a different subject. The child has eyes and ears formed by nature to mark and observe all. Those optics which open with an instinctive knowledge of the language of facts and deeds, are gifted with a noble, natural independence, which makes them scorn professions of a contradictory nature made in a deceptive language. Often does the incautious parent fall under this censure in the eye of a child whose discrimination he discredits, but which, infantile as it is, sees his inconsistences clearly.

And if parents thus sometimes educate their darling offspring to a practical disregard of the principles of truth and right, what evil lessons may they not receive. from observing the conduct of the vicious and corrupt, to whose influence the children of the poor are often greatly exposed! In a moral and religious point of view, therefore, Infant Schools must prove of inestimable benefit to that class. Without them many of the little wretched ones would never have either a good precept or a virtuous example presented to them, from one year's end to another. On the contrary, they would be regularly trained to sin and crime.

On every account, therefore, the Infant School is an object worthy of the highest attention to the intelligent traveller; for in some way or other its principles may be beneficially applied to every branch of education, private and public.

In the United States we have specimens of education in all degrees, from the universal, the all-pervad-
ing system of Connecticut, to the want of system and
want of means observed in our most distant and
ignorant new settlements. In the state just mentioned,
the first habitations were erected in 1634, and in a few
years a law made it the duty of town officers to visit
every family frequently, and fine parents and guardians
who should be found neglecting the instruction of their
children and wards. The state is now divided into
school districts, in each of which a free school is kept,
and the whole of the expense is defrayed from the
interest of the school fund, which amounts to nearly
two millions. The same spirit is found to have dicta-
ted the early institutions of the other New-England
states, the influence of which has long been proverbial, and which have been justly regarded a necessary
material in the foundation of the enterprise and flourishing condition of that part of the country. In Rhode-
Island, the want of a general system of education
has been deeply felt, and long been made the theme
of reproach, which there is now reason to believe will
soon be wiped away. New-York, although not enjoying the same advantages in institutions early established, and in a population of the most favorable kind,
has distinguished herself in her recent and devoted
attachment to the cause of useful knowledge, and
done, perhaps, what no other state could have been
expected to do in her situation. In New-England
education will ever be adhered to with the pertinacity
of a rooted but honest prejudice : in New-York it has
been adopted from a reasonable regard to its benefits,

and from a liberal sacrifice of old habits. A rivalry seems to be arising between different states, to obtain and secure power and importance of an intellectual nature ; and this is one of the most gratifying views in which the legislation of our union can be examined. Here is an epitome of the world, to some extent : and the contest between knowledge and ignorance is going on, at its different stages, on a number of arenas almost as large as the number of the states. The facilities which aid the progress of knowledge in some parts of the country, and the various obstacles it has to encounter in others, offer us instructive subjects for reflection ; and the study of them would not be made at a waste of time.

Comparing the east and the south, we see the value of a compact village population, above that of the plantation system ; and the ease with which a good plan might be set into operation among a people prepared for it by an orderly and moral state of society ; while we perceive the difficulties and discouragements which must follow the application of our system to the south. ern regions of the Union. If experiments are fairly to be made, they ought to be made at the east ; and it is to attract the attention of good and judicious people to what may be done, that I am making the present remarks. The state of Connecticut, as before ob. served, has the best plan for general education in operation. If free schools for all classes are any where to be established, they ought to be established on some similar one. I now speak only in reference to the division of the territory into small districts, sup. plying them with schools in the reach of all, and allowing every child access. The son of the merest vagabond may there find admission. If he has no other shelter to resort to, he has a right to a seat in the place of instruction, guaranteed him by law, and a legal claim on the same words of instruction that others derive from the lips of the teacher. My wish is, that these advantages should be greater ; and in a few words it might be shown where and what improvements are necessary.

Yet with all the excellency of its intention and the universality of the plan, the effects which ought to be produced by this system are limited within narrow bounds. Every child is instructed, but the share of each is small. The plan on which the schools are conducted is founded on the erroneous, tardy and inefficient principles before mentioned. And it happens as a peculiar misfortune, that in that state where the organization appears at first view to be the most complete, there is an absence of a general controlling power. The state has never assumed the authority of directing the plan of instruction, which has been exercised by the individual towns. No plan for improvement therefore in the general system of school instruction in Connecticut is supposed to be in the power of their legislature. Persons ignorant of a better system, or satisfied with the old one, must be convinced in great numbers and probably by a slow process, before the towns would yield up what some of them regard as their proper right. It is not always an easy task to convince an individual that a new plan should be adopted ; and the number is quite formidable of those who have to be persuaded before they will concur.

We may therefore probably see a general reformation first commenced in other states; and if our legislatures appreciated the importance of the subject, there would be a strong rivalry among them for the honor of leading the way in so enlightened and advantageous a course. Under a general view, education presents a source of prime and acknowledged importance still in its infancy, though in the midst of a people who owe to it more than any other: without which political institutions like those we enjoy can no where exist unless in name, and but for which we could not possess for two generations. The objects of education are in general defined, and its effects appreciated so far as they are seen; but the system, with all its extent and benefits, moves with antiquated and incompetent machinery. The ingenuity of our countrymen has conversed with every branch of art, but on this great science it has not distinguished itself. In investigating its true principles, no combined plan has been produced and no practical hand has been extended to arrange or to put them in operation. And this remark may be extended to the whole world. There are countless multitudes who are interested in the subject; but teachers and learners are like a group of blind men, who can go only as far as they are led. Whoever would write the history of this science, must confine himself to solitary exertions made by individuals—repeated inventions, wasted on the first stages of the subject. Teachers and parents, from time immemorial, have exhausted their ingenuity

on the mere alphabet of the science ; and their discoveries, being unrecorded, have all in turn been disused
and required to be rediscovered by their successors.
The points arrived at by some, have no doubt been
important ; but they have perished almost as soon as
ascertained. There is no depository for useful inventions in this important branch ; the models decay, and
the principles are forgotten.

There is one plant in the world, the proper culture
of which is no where understood ; and it is that which
is known to be of longest life, and noblest qualities ;
capable of attaining greater perfection and of being
raised to higher perfections than any other ; liable to
suffer more from neglect and able more richly to repay
the care of the cultivator ; indigenous in all climates,
able to endure every variety of situation, soil and sky.
This plant of celestial origin and immortal destiny,
destined to flourish side by side with the amaranth,
where does it enjoy an estimation corresponding with
its exalted nature ? How often do we see it despised
and neglected ! The learned, the ingenious, the great
in what is called science, devote their attention even
to the most insignificant and useless plants, train them
with care and assiduity, and study out their habits and
peculiarities ; and with how meagre a reward of a few
insipid facts do they content themselves for their toil !
How lamentable a comment this on their own early
education !

It is as yet too early to obtain many long or satisfactory anecdotes concerning Infant Schools, except

such as the teachers or the founders might relate, concerning the character of some of the pupils, or the abodes of poverty from which they have proceeded. showing the inheritance of wretchedness, ignorance. and vice to which they were born legitimate heirs : but they cannot yet present an individual's mind on whom this noble system of early culture has been fully tried, lay before us each quality of the heart. every faculty of the soul which has felt its invigorating influence, and show how different would have been the result but for such an interference. Much less can they look forward so far as to predict, what a bearing it may hereafter have on the intellectual and moral condition of the country, or even of a single individual. One who has witnessed the operation of the system, even in a single instance, must, it would seem, inevitably fall into reflections of a very interesting nature. He will see that a machine has been applied to the infantile mind, the effect of which he can perceive to some extent, without having ever felt it in his own case. That it must be vast, he has the sagacity to anticipate : but to limit or describe it he dares not. restricted and crippled as are his powers under the tutelage of an imperfect, and in some respects a vicious system.

Without entering into one of the numerous fancies in which an enthusiastic imagination might be tempted to indulge on the consideration of this system, it may not be entirely uninteresting, to give a short account of the progress of one little child in the brief career he has thus far had an opportunity to pursue in one of our Infant Schools. He was born to such

poverty, that after some weeks had been spent in preparation by his mother, the best suit she could find to
array him in was so poor, that it would have debarred
his entrance almost any where else. He surveyed
the apartment, the teachers, the pupils and the appara-
tus with mingled apprehension, hope, and doubt. Up
to that moment of his life, as it would appear, no one
had ever taken the pains to instruct him in any thing
useful: his parents, like many of the poor, and not a
few of the rich, appeared to have exerted themselves
to control him only so far as was convenient; he had
been a close though silent observer of the degraded
manners and vicious practices which are continually
passing before the eyes in many of the narrow and
crowded streets of the city, and was learning to
semble, after the example of those around him,
and even that of his parents, who would persuade
him with false promises, or terrify him with bugbears,
as best suited their temporary convenience. He had
heard of the criminality of falsehood, but he had
seen it resorted to by his best friends, as the means
of securing their own interests. Those around
him had sometimes spoken of duty and religion, of
death, a future world, and perhaps a saviour: but
none had ever appeared to think these mighty subjects
of importance to him, or within the compass of his
understanding. His curiosity had often been awakened about things which he knew existed, by some of
those evidences which lead even children's thoughts
to consider unseen objects; his heart had been impressed with the importance of truths of which he
would fain have learned something; and all this at a

period of life when perchance he could not have framed a question aright concerning the subject he would have pried into. There had been none to anticipate these natural longings of the mind, there was none who appreciated its tendency or its capacity; and he had begun to sink into that listlessness and torpor of the intellect, which necessarily seizes on a mind thus early discouraged in its attempts to proceed, and barred out from every avenue to knowledge.

How many lovely children are there in such a lamentable condition on all sides of us! How many are there, (let the rich and the learned as well as the poor and the ignorant, ask themselves the question,) who seek in vain that support and nurture for their youthful minds which they require, and which it is so unparental as well as irreparably injurious to withhold:—even among that class of our countrymen who enjoy every facility for training up their children in the way they should go, and who fancy they do almost a work of supererogation when they condescend occasionally to inquire into the progress of their children, of their tutors; how many are there who devote not one-half the attention or money to their early instruction, which they bestow in consulting their vanity in dress or their whims in eating. But it is in vain to waste lamentations on what is as little likely to be amended in the education of young children, as any of the great and fundamental errors and abuses which prevail in the whole plan of what is termed the fashionable bringing up of their elders. To the eye

of a human observer, ignorant of what was in preparation for little helpless beings like him, this boy would
have appeared destined to that ignorance of moral,
intellectual and religious truths, by which as a standard so many of us are ready to measure the conduct
of the despised and neglected poor. But Providence,
for him, as for not a few like him, had richer gifts in
store.   When I entered that abode of peace, harmony,
knowledge, and happiness—the Infant School, he, in
his little coarse suit, stood on the elevated stage to
which his merits and application had promoted him;
his meek but intelligent eyes cast on the ground, his
little hands clasped in decorum, and his humble lips
beginning to repeat the hymn which had been assign-
ed for morning worship.   More than two hundred
little ones, whom the same charity had sought out in
abodes almost as miserable as that in which she had
found him, stood in similar attitudes around the room;
while one of their number, who surpassed in intelligence all but the humble hero of this humble story,
from a station of secondary distinction caught from
his lips the solemn words he had uttered, and then
joined with his musical voice in the peal of infantile
harmony which, the next moment, resounded from all
sides.   In all the lessons, he was leader of two hundred.

   Thus far has one individual proceeded in this new
course of instruction ; and in the mean time hundreds
of others have not been idle. Every closing day marks
the progressive improvement of many a little mind in
useful knowledge, which, by an increasing ratio, may
in time proceed beyond the bound that even its in-

structors would fix. And all this is doing, let the fond and fashionable mother remember, while the nurselings of her flock are perhaps left in that state of ignorance, to which many a promising child is condemned, through a total misconception, or a criminal despite of those capacities with which it has been endowed by the hand of its Creator.

THE WHITE MOUNTAINS.

The view from the little inn at Conway, embraces the first, and probably the last general display of all the vast features of the White Mountains, which will be presented to the traveller approaching them from the south. Here he seems to have reached the gates of a vast avenue, bounded on either hand by mountains of great elevation, and terminating in a region where the pale blue peaks penetrate the clouds, and sometimes bear them on their breasts, showing that nature has there concentrated all the magnificence and sublimity of this district. Sometimes those distant and pre-eminent summits stand out clear of the mists and vapours ; but as they are in a region rarely free from clouds, it is but seldom that they are distinctly visible.

The seasons present different phenomena on their sides and pinnacles. The snows by which they are invested during eight or nine months of the year, assume various degrees of light and shadow, from the different directions in which they are struck by the beams of the sun ; and the dazzling rays which they sometimes pour back in reflection, seem as if they

had been rejected from a surface of polished steel.—
To the eye of a novice, however, the most singular
and unaccountable appearance is sometimes perceiv.
ed, when the greater part of the mountains are divested of the snow, and only a mass or two remain
to reflect the light of the sun. This dazzling glare
is then rendered doubly striking by the contrast of the
colour of the mountains; and the stranger often seeks
in vain to account for so singular a phenomenon. No
one, it may be boldly affirmed, unacquainted with
similar scenes, would be prepared for so brillant a
reflection from a body of snow at so great a distance;
and when a light cloud intervenes, as is often the case,
with a veil just sufficient to hide the mountain, while
the gleam is distinctly perceptible, from its undefined
form, and its apparent independence of every terres.
trial thing, it seems almost like a supernatural light.

It is not until the traveller beholds a general view
of the mountains, like that presented from this spot.
that he can fully appreciate the magnificent character
of the region he is now entering; and but for the ad.
vantage of seeing such a display, a great part of the
pleasure of the excursion would to many persons be
lost. From this spot onward, objects are to be scruti-
nized in detail; and as each mountain can be referred
to its appropriate place, while the memory of this
sight is preserved, and each be regarded according
to its comparative importance in the general scale,
what is seen will be constantly reminding us of what
is unseen, which must necessarily be the greater part
of the whole.

The Saco River, which flows in a graceful course

through the level valley that forms the foreground of this scene, may be imagined to have come, as it in fact does come, from that high and remarkable summit to which our sight almost fails to reach—Mount Washington; and it may be conjectured what romantic regions, what shady valleys, what retired caverns, what headlong precipices it has visited in its passage. Within the distance it has traversed, smooth and undisturbed as it here appears, it has made a descent of perhaps four thousand feet; and as the traveller pursues the rough road which sagaciously threads out its devious course, like a wily serpent, through the long passes of the mountains, he will have frequent cause to admire its numerous rapids and waterfalls.

In different parts of this widely extended plain before us, are however to be seen piles of timber and heaps of sand and stones, thrown up by the stream during an extraordinary inundation which occurred in the White Mountains in the month of August, 1826. The marks of this flood are still to be seen in a great many places, and some are of such a nature that nothing less than a similar exertion of the elements can ever obliterate them. A great portion of this level was for a time overflown; and the immense loads of uprooted trees and shattered branches which were thrown into the stream by the ruin of the forests above, were borne down and deposited here, in situations far from its present course, and at an elevation which it would seem impossible it should ever have reached. The stream of the Saco, seen in its ordinary state during the summer months, strikes us as it might to see a giant in the decrepitude of extreme old age, when we reflect with astonishment, and almost with incredulity, on the height to which it once attained, and witness the proofs of the extraordinary power it once exerted.

These are the first marks of that great catastrophe the traveller observes in coming from the south, although they are visible many miles towards the east, for here he first meets the Saco. As he proceeds he will find them multiplied and magnified, till his admiration at the scenes of ruin in his path will exceed all bounds.

The first explorers of one of the rivers of South America, if I recollect aright, were shocked at the sight of its waters, which flowed to the coast dyed, by certain plants upon its margin, with the redness of blood; and with mingled feelings of curiosity and pain, traced out its course with the expectation of arriving at some recent field of battle. Thus as we proceed up the valley of the Saco, amidst the solitudes through which it flows, though objects of beauty abound, and many a little woodland scene opens upon us to captivate the eye, we are impressed by these marks of destruction with an awful idea of the wreck we are soon to witness. But in this case there is no agreeable surprise to await us, for the impressions become more powerful at every turn, till we find ourselves in the desolation of what was created desolate, and the rude commingling of vast objects, which were before awful for size, and ranged without form or order. And the nearer we approach to the centre of devastation, the more do we yield ourselves up to the feelings of astonishment which the scene so naturally inspires.

When we meet, in a mountainous country, with those contrasts of beauty and wildness, gentleness and sublimity, which such regions generally present : the majesty and awfulness of the wide forest, the naked summit, the prone rock, and the overhanging precipice, make us the more admire and enjoy the rich valleys at their feet, and the calmness and coolness of the streams which water them. The feelings of sublimity become painful, after they have been long excited by the view of vast magnitudes, and useless extensions of height, depth, or level surface ; but they are often relieved by our recurring to milder, calmer, and more encouraging objects, with which we generally find them intermingling. The comforts of a cottage, the pleasant aspect of a river's margin, the green nibbled turf under the shade of a grove, alternately administer to us a calm which alleviates the painful exertion we make in contemplating things too great for our powers. But when all gentler features are removed from the scene, it produces feelings that we should not choose to experience for a long time, at least without some intermission.

The Notch House, as it is popularly called, has ever been one of the spots most agreeable to the recollection of a traveller through the White Mountains, as the only shelter afforded within a distance of sixteen miles, as the only place where the hand of cultivation and the works of man presented a gentle and tranquilizing contrast to the vast and sublime objects of nature. This building, which many a weary and many an almost perishing traveller has welcomed with joy—situated in the midst of a little plain, highly verdant in the warmer season, enclosed by lofty mountains, most of them wooded to their summits, shut out from every violent wind, and exposed at mid-day to the full heat of the sun ; this little valley may be remembered by those who have passed it only at such periods, like those imaginary retreats in tropical countries, the beauties of which have been described in glowing language. Far other, however, has been its aspect to most of those acquainted with these regions. At no great distance from the house, a rising ground brings to the mind the melancholy fate of a young woman, who here terminated an enterprise to which she was incited by an ardent and faithful attachment to her distant lover ; and every one who passes the place while the mountains are invested with snow, realizes that he also might be exposed to certain death but for the relief provided in this hospitable retreat. Being applied to the same humane purpose as the solitary monasteries and stranger's houses on the Alps, the Andes, &c. it excites similar feelings in the traveller who seeks its aid, in the dreary months of the long winter, when nature presents only an aspect fierce and relentless to man. He feels that he is to contest for life, against the blast that would freeze the blood in his veins, as it has covered the mountains with snow and the valleys with ice, and whose power seems illimitable. The following is from the notes of a traveller :

"The recollections I entertain of that spot are at once delightful and terrific, as a change of the atmosphere presented the objects around under two differ-

'ent aspects. After a slow passage through the gorge of the mountain, during which, being alone, I stopped more frequently to admire, and I spent more time than I was then sensible of, this beautiful valley unexpectedly opened to view, with its smooth plain, once cultivated and not at first discovered to be neglected, with the venerable old house standing near the road. My horse, my only companion, was soon placed in the barn, the emptiness of which I remarked without conjecturing the cause ; and it was not until I stepped into the door, and heard a swallow fly over my head, that I imagined myself to be still alone. The rooms were empty : no furniture was to be seen, excepting one or two large bedsteads, where weary travellers had doubtless found welcome repose. The great fireplace was cold, and a late rain had sent many a drop down the chimney. But where they had fallen lay a heap of ashes and a half-burnt log of great size, the fire from which had added to the dingy color of the walls, and probably supplied some party of travellers, long since scattered, with comfort and cheerfulness for a winter evening. The windows which the hail storm had probably gradually deprived of glass, had been partly closed by boards rudely nailed over the vacant sashes ; so that the light which was but imperfectly admitted, impressed me with the idea that the day was far spent. As I proceeded from room to room, the darkness seemed to increase ; and as I knew that it was not past noon, I went to the door to satisfy myself whether my eyes had deceived me. But I found the whole valley deeply shaded by a cloud, which had concealed the sun almost as soon as it had come over the mountain ; and a few trees on the upper peaks were the only objects on which the light now fell. The darkness spread around was as deep as that of approaching evening, and the bright spots above might have been taken for those of sunset ; but the general aspect of things was of a more sorrowful and portentous nature. A sudden roar, apparently at no great distance, attracted my attention to the tops of the mountain behind me, which, like that rising opposite, was covered with a thick vestment of forest trees, from the base to the summit. The upper region was wrapped in the dense cloud, through which nothing was visible ; and just in the advance of it the tops of the trees were violently waving to and fro, as if pressed by an irresistible tempest. Some of the branches seemed to separate from their trunks ; but the cloud moved so rapidly down towards me and followed so hard upon the blast that preceded it, that it was impossible to ascertain any of its effects. Indeed the approach was so fast, and the roaring became so much louder, that I began to question whether the old house would be safe in such a tempest. In an another instant, a loud rattling on the roof persuaded me that hail stones were falling ; and the long blades of grass and the large leaves of plants began to drop here and there. I stepped to the barn, half resolved to lead my horse into the open air, and there encounter the storm unsheltered, rather than incur the risk of more serious injury ; and half compassionating my faithful animal, which, I had no doubt, felt as much the want of a companion as myself. I found him in a great alarm, starting at the redoubled noise now caused by the fall of a

severe shower, and endeavortng to obtain his freedom
by force; and no small exertions were necessary to
quiet his fears, and to control him so far as to enable
me to look at leisure on the scene around.

"The gust had passed rapidly by, closely followed by
the large drops of rain, which seemed to prostrate
every blade of grass they touched, and were dashed
with such violence upon the ground, that they threw
up a thin mist of spray. In a moment every thing
was hidden from view, and we were in the midst of a
shower which might remind a traveller of those so
common in the Gulf Stream. The landscape however
soon began to appear on all sides, as the cloud passed
rapidly by; and just as the sun began again to shine
around, the roar of the gust once more attracted
my attention, raving among the forests which clothed
the side of the mountain that impended over the opposite side of the valley, and involving them in turn in
shade and confusion. The wind tore off the long
pendants of moss, which hung on the boughs of the
venerable old hemlocks, like mourning weeds displayed
for the ages they had seen depart; and the slender
poplars shrunk at its approach, and tossed their white
arms in vain.

"Before we were again on the way, the storm had
passed beyond the view; and when I stopped on
the rising ground where the road re-enters the forest,
the whole valley was of the same bright green as
before, and the trees that invested the mountains on
either hand were as calm as if no such scene of tumult
had ever visited that lonely retreat. But a tremendous catastrophe has since occurred. The house has

been inhabited, but is now more desolate than ever. The family who had their home there in 1826, warned by one or two avalanches, caused, as is supposed, by the drought of two seasons followed by drenching rains, had prepared a little retreat at a short distance ; and alarmed by a tremendous sound one night, left their beds, and were probably making their way for it in the dark, when they found a watery grave." The public are acquainted with many of the circumstances of this event. No person was left alive to tell the tale. When the sun arose the next day, it witnessed alone the effects of the storm. The Saco had risen to with-in a short distance of the house ; on the other side two avalanches had come down, in the direction of the shower above described : and one proceeding with its awful crash and tremendous chaotic roar, towards the dwelling, being turned a little to the south, proba-bly by a slight irregularity of the ground, had rolled some of its rocks and trunks of trees to within three feet of the walls, and stopped without producing any injury. The other had taken the garden and the barn in its track ; and but a vestige of them was to be found. The hut which the inhabitants had pre-pared, would have afforded no refuge. Though the spot was chosen as the safest, it was merged beneath the lake that had risen in a few moments and covered the valley, while some of the domestic animals, by retreating from the barn, had found safety near the house. All the calculations of prudence seem to have been set at nought in this war of the elements, as all human power and exertions would have appeared contemptible if they could have been brought to resist

Avalanches in the White Mountains.

Sketched by D.Wadsworth Esqr.

it, and as the feelings of man are put to their stretch by the contemplation of the effects. Such a mass of ruin strews the valley, and so incredible has been the dilapidation of the mountains, that we are at a loss to conjecture what number of ages could ever restore the scene to its former appearance, while we despair to communicate by a description any idea of its present condition. From the spot whence the traveller looked back, to admire the green meadow below, and the crowds of forest trees which invested the mountains, unbroken except here and there by a few gray rocks, the avalanches I have mentioned are all visible, each of them a course which no human power could have resisted, and before which the pyramids of Egypt might have have been shaken if not swept away. Not only this, but about one hundred other avalanches have channelled the mountains on either hand, scraping off every tree from their summits and their sides, and tearing away the soil to the rocks which it had covered since the creation, leaving cheerless ridges of impenetrable granite exposed, on which scarcely a green blade or leaf is to be discovered; while the timber and the earth that have thus been removed, lie in a chaos over the plain, or are scattered for twenty or thirty miles below, along the course of the Saco. The annexed lithographic print will give a correct idea of the singular appearance of the avalanches of that mountain up which the shower ascended; as it is from a drawing made by a gentleman distinguished for his taste and accuracy, who visited the spot a few months after the

7

catastrophe.   The observer stands among the avalanches which fell behind the Notch House.

The mists which rise from moist places, and assume such a variety of form and appearance, are among the most striking accompaniments of the scenery of the White Mountains.   It may be left for the investigation of the curious and scientific, to discover by what causes they are often made to appear in a spot which the moment before has been observed or visited by the traveller, in the enjoyment of pure air and sunshine : and to ascertain why the atmosphere is affected by the changeable and freakish currents by which the vapors are moved, now up, now strait forward, now quickly, now slowly ; and by what variations of temperature they are so suddenly thickened, divided and dissolved.   The traveller seeks in vain to account for those phenomena, on any of the ordinary principles by which mists are regulated in other situations ; and his mind is not more baffled in attempts to ascertain the causes, than are his steps in avoiding, or his eyes in pursuing them.   His attention he will often find aroused, his curiosity excited ; and probably feelings of solemnity, if not almost of superstition, will croud upon him, as he sees his path suddenly hidden in a mist, as dense as that which Venus threw around Æneas at Carthage, and finds himself involved in a shade which his eyes cannot penetrate ; or is startled by a shadow passing over neighboring objects, and observes what seems a moody figure, shrouded in white, with face averted and bowed head ; moving silently and solemnly up the side of a mountain—or a column of heavy form rising perpendicularly to a great height, and suddenly dissipated into nothing.

too great almost for the caves to endure, or the echoes to repeat; and the result lies around and below us.

When I passed along these regions in early times, the hours I lost and knew not how, were spent in measuring the altitudes above, the magnitudes at any side, and the depths below. I tried to form ideas of their dimensions, by imagining some of the most magnificent structures I had ever seen upon their tops ; or some of those cities which are visited on account of their grandeur and magnificence, constructed on their sides ; and while considering a vast tract of forest, which had been burnt over by a fire that left the trunks of the trees standing, I estimated how large a portion of those thousand acres would remain, if all the navies of Europe were represented by hemlocks corresponding in number, (though exceeding in size,) with their stately masts.

Now, standing on a shelf against the rock where the road once ran, and looking down in the gulf far beneath, the spectator may begin by reflecting on the most gigantic means of injury used by man, and comparing them with what he sees. Here is a rock rounded like a cannon shot—see what a trench it has made in the earth, where it struck with the velocity it had acquired in falling from an immense height.— There lies a mass of granite, as large as the stone balls thrown by Turkish cannon in the Dardanelles, one of which is sufficient to sink a frigate, and perhaps tear a merchantman in two. Yonder lies the rock from which it dropped off, like a pebble or a grain of sand, if that be compared to the size of a common

dwelling for one of our pigmy race ; next it is a palace.
and yonder a whole city in ruins.

A long period of unusual drought, succeeded by
several weeks of continued rain, is supposed to have
prepared for the terrible catastrophe, by destroying
or enfeebling the roots of the trees, loosening the
earth in some places, undermining rocks in others,
saturating the loose soil with water, and making the sub-
terranean caverns repositories of an immense hydros-
tatic power.   Such had been the nature of the season ;
and, while the country was in that condition, the sudden bursting of a tremendous deluge from the clouds,
sufficient almost to crush to the ground every tree on
which it fell, could not have failed to produce extensive results.   But it must be acknowledged that the
effects, when viewed on the spot, appear to have been
altogether too universal, and too instantaneous even
for such causes.   Whatever they may have been
owing to, however, these effects are such that man
must as long labour to surmount them as to explain
the way in which they have been produced.

There was a little stream that poured in a long current down the steep side of a mountain, and rushing
by among broken rocks, passed tumultuously beneath
my feet, at a place where the road had been constructed, with long and persevering industry, across its
wild and precipitate course.   I was struck with delight at the first glimpse of the scene, and broke into
expressions of new surprise and pleasure, as I traced
its gleams far up above me.   It washed the feet of a
thousand venerable and gigantic trees ; while, along
the little grassy margin below, the annual flowers that

could endure the climate, presented their little blossoms every season, although they could have experienced only weeks of sunshine for months of snow. By the chance of some gust, they had been planted in one of the most genial little spots in the mountains; and there seemed to have taken up their abode in contentment, like the innocent and secluded family, which last taught the valley to repeat the praise of the Almighty. And how like theirs is the fate they have since endured! Many a traveller will remember with pleasure this beautiful spot; but who can draw or even describe the richness of the cascade in its upper regions, where, in a stronger light, it seemed like the dropping of dew from the leaves over head, or the distilling of a pure balsam from the boughs of an evergreen by which the road was shaded. Perhaps the rude memorial I have of it, in a little sketch hastily drawn, is the only one now in existence. Ten thousand tons of massy rock have since swept with terrific crash along the place where I stood; and not only the bridge and the road, but acres of forest trees, along with the earth which supported them, have rushed into a gulf on the other side, down which I had looked almost with shuddering.

There was a spot on the Ammonoosuc where I spent a few solitary hours in fishing, and which has shared largely in the general desolation. The banks of the stream were at that time marked by rows of tall forest trees, which presented to the eye an avenue, as it wandered up the current, to see whence proceeded all the uproar and dashing. The shades on either hand could hardly have been more impenetrable if

they had been composed of walls of solid stone, instead of the living vegetation; and the roof formed
over head by the arms of the immense trees, would
not have made a more complicated tracery, if it
had belonged to the arches of a Gothic edifice. The
rapid stream came hurrying through, as if it had just
escaped from some irksome confinement, and was
soon to pass by and subside. My horse started, as if
struck by a musket ball, when he first heard the tumult; and I, though less quick of ear, could never
divest my mind of the impression, that I saw something more tumultuous than ordinary. Yet, go when
you would, hour after hour, year after year, and perhaps century after century, (for so did the deeply
channelled rocks testify,) it was unaltered; and
though it appeared always the same, like passing time,
was making all haste to be gone, and seemed to be
rushing on for some mysterious object.

Now, how changed the scene! an overwhelming
flood has visited the spot, which drowned the very
cataract itself. The trees were uprooted, the earth
deeply wounded in her bosom, even below the depth to
which the long roots descended; the rocks were not
worn away, but removed, and the ruins lie scattered
and mouldering for miles down the course of the
stream. The venerable old hemlock, which stood
dressed in a drapery of moss, the testimony of its
antiquity, is now gone, and has left no monument of
itself.

Thus in wild and mountainous scenes like those,
does nature sometimes sternly forbid the approach of
man. There are regions in all quarters of the world
which seem designed for eternal solitude; and so

like are they in their great characteristics, that, for all the purposes of the traveller, he is as well in the White Mountains as in the lower ranges of the Alps or the Appennines. The works of nature alone are seen : every thing is removed which indicates the artificial differences of different countries, and leaves the visiter to feel like a citizen of the world. The generalizing of the term Alpine, therefore, appears peculiarly appropriate. Similar elevation renders it so : as the human mind, when exalted to a height but seldom attained, claims a kindred with all who are called great, or have been, or shall be. These regions, like the wild beasts which inhabit them, recognise not even the existence of society ; and while they have never heard of the blessings of wise laws, and refined institutions, such as we boast of in our republic, are also free from the oppression of absolute power. Man is excluded by the rigors of the climate, and the sterility of the soil ; and government and the endearments of society go not a step beyond him. When we see the torrent's path, and the devastation of the avalanche, we regard nature, in her more majestic and awful aspect as the enemy of civilization and humanity. She appears, as she does on the ocean, to delight only in waste and destruction. But when we reflect again, the broad sheets of untrodden snow that cap or zone the mountains above us, appear like emblems of nature's purity, who in her most secluded temples, cannot endure misery or crime ; and from these scenes repels man and his concerns together.

When a visiter to the White Mountains begins to get involved among the peculiar scenery which de. notes his approach to those magnificent regions, every feature of nature seems to partake of the same general wildness. The rocks overhang, the hills look darker, more uncultivated and more inaccessible, the music of singing birds gives place to the discordant notes of birds of prey, and the streams hurry by in a wild and impetuous manner, while the marks of devastation along their banks show with how rude a hand they often brush away the shrubs and flowers, the fields, and sometimes the habitations of men. They seem to partake of the wild and untameable disposition of the savage beasts which drink at their fountains; and when the dashing of their boisterous waters unexpectedly assails the ear of the traveller, he instinctively starts as if a wolf had howled.

Far up the course of one of those wildest streams, however, and almost immediately on its bank, a family not many years since were found to have taken up their abode, among whom dwelt a degree of refinement seldom to be seen in more genial regions, and where prevailed a degree of domestic tranquillity and happiness which formed a strong moral contrast with the unceasing turmoil and lawless violence which filled the little valley with loud though inarticulate murmurs. Much might the traveller wonder to find an oft-read Shakspeare lying at hand on the sofa on which he rested himself, and to hear that Scott's admirers were not wanting in so retired and solitary a region. Such, however is the force of education generally diffused among a population well gifted by

nature ; and when, in situations like these, intellectual
refinement is found connected with religious feelings,
the character of man appears to suffer less in the comparison with what is great and sublime in the inani-
mate works of creation. The severe atmosphere and
the sterile soil of a mountainous district, usually degrade the mind as much as they beggar the body in
other countries ; but in our own, where poverty, hap-
pily, is not an insurmountable barrier to education,
and where schools and books are almost as general
and free as the rain, there are fewer impediments to
prevent the poor from some portion of learning, and
not solitary instances of cultivated minds in the most
unfavourable situations.

From individuals of this character the traveller
may sometimes obtain descriptions of the varying aspects of the earth and the sky in seasons when he
cannot visit these mountains, and bear away with him
impressions of scenes which few except the fixed inhabitants of such regions ever witness :—the appearance of those storms which sweep round the cliffs and
through the almost uninhabitable valleys, the purity
of the rude surface when covered with a sheet of
snow, that bears only the track of the deer, the bear,
the wolf, or the catamount; the roar of the deluge
which pours through the valleys when the rains fall
and the sun melts the frost ; the spectacles produced
by masses of ice broken like the walls of a marble
prison, borne rapidly down by the roaring streams, or
heaped in piles upon the land. The aspects of nature
as seen by them from their humble casements, and
often by them alone, are worthy of description, and

interesting to the contemplation: the furious storm that works its wild will among those immeasurable regions of desolation—the sunshine, the clouds, the moon, the stars, with all their variety of grandeur and beauty.

NEW SPECIES OF TRAVELLERS.

A PERSON who has before passed over our principal routes, but now resumes his journeying after the intermission of a few years, will meet with new personages, novel modes and strange features, in some of those he sees. There are, mingled among our travelling groupes, faces embrowned by the sun of the equator, by the winds that sweep from the Andes down the shores of Peru, by the burning heats of the Spanish-Maine, (now the coast of Colombia,) and the complexion of the Mexican, colored with his own gold. The man of retirement who has not before come in contact with these strangers, is naturally astonished at seeing these indications of changes in the condition of the southern countries of America, which he has been but generally informed of. He naturally reflects that he has not appreciated as they deserved the events which have so fundamentally affected the vital interests of millions of his fellow-creatures. He has read of the treasure and blood expended during the few past years, to liberate them from the oppression of a cruel and superstitious monarchy ; but it is not

8

until he sees some of them face to face, and feels them
grasp his hand, that he begins to think the purchase
has been cheaply effected ; nor until he has compared
himself with them—mind to mind, heart to heart—
until he has admired their native genius, contem.
plated their refinement and taste, and witnessed the
flow of their ardent feelings, cherished under the tro.
pical or meridian sun, that he reflects that more bril.
liant minds and more generous hearts than he had
imagined, have been released from a despotic thrall
by the happy result of their struggles for indepen.
dence.

With what animation does such a stranger dilate
upon the beauties of that country he has left to visit
our own ; how does the majesty of our mountains sink
before his descriptions of the vast Andes, their breasts
loaded with gold and their summits with snow; how
fertile his native valleys, how extensive those plains,
to which our most favorite scenes serve but as mate.
rials for amplification ; and how poetical are the
visions, and yet perhaps how real, which he indulges
in, when he marks with admiration the success of our
arts and enterprise, and enumerates the hundreds of
leagues traversed by his rivers, and the luxuriance
with which nature has enriched their shores! He
opens to our view a new world, of which our best
geographers and historians, our naturalists and philo.
sophers, are profoundly ignorant, even in their appropriate departments ; and while with South American
animation, and more than what is commonly supposed
to be South American refinement, he sketches to us
the varying situation, climate, and productions of hill.

vale and mountain, whose melodious names are new
to our ears, and whose delightful situations are unknown to our maps, we are disposed to lend full cre-
dence to what we have heard of the talents of the
extemporaneous poets of our twin continent. He tells
us of the almost endless courses of those rivers,
which are able to weary the very steam-paddles by
which they are destined soon to be familiarly explored;
the impenetrable forests which line many leagues
along their banks ; the luxuriant vegetation to which
they afford support ; the extensive vallies which are
enclosed by the Andes, at different elevations—some
scorched by the unmitigated rays of the equatorial
sun; some desolated by moving clouds of ravenous
insects ; some continually menaced by volcanos
which occasionally pour forth ruin in its most terrible
forms; and others traversed by healthful and fertiliz-
ing streams, elevated to situations where they enjoy
a temperate climate. He depicts to us the conditions
and the exigences of a numerous population, con-
gregated in cities of which we know not even the
names, surrounded by fruitful fields, and distinguished
as seats of learning. He tells of individuals whose
talents have been cherished in some of the few institutions, which, in spite of Spanish oppression, grew
up in those secluded corners of the earth, of men, who,
holding no communication with the enlightened of
their species, except through such books as found
their way to their retirement, investigated the wonders and beauties of nature in the magnificent displays
around them; and of those who, actuated as if by a spontaneous and independent influence, meditated on the

means of confering intellectual and moral blessings
on their country—and not unfreqûently alludes to
their tragical end, and the losses which the world has
suffered through the extinguishing of such lights as
burst out in the darkest places.

We listen with attention to narrations like these;
and then it is that we feel how important is the change
which has taken place in the political condition of
South America ; and realize that liberty has, as it
were, performed again the part of Columbus, and rediscovered that continent to the world.

To enjoy the society of such an individual on a tour
of pleasure, is a high gratification. It gives a new
interest to familiar scenes, and excites in a good degree those feelings in our hearts which he expresses
with such warmth. We have the advantage also of
viewing every thing in a contrast, generally agreeable,
and always instructive. However much and however
justly he may dwell upon the natural beauties of his
land, he concludes his descriptions of them with high
commendations of our political and social advantages,
of which he seems, by a kind of instinct, to appreciate
the excellences, if he cannot at once penetrate to all
the causes. In the operation of our political system,
our habits, and our moral, literary and religious institutions, he contemplates the motions of a vast machine,
of which the great results alone he before had witnessed. He views with admiration the arrangement
and co-operation of all the parts, being sensible, from
the experience of his own countrymen in their legis-
lative councils, that many qualities are essentially
necessary in the plan, in the construction and even in

every material, the want of any one of which might impede the motion, and perhaps cause the ruin of the whole. He inspects the population, he studies the customs and the feelings of the people, he puts to us discriminating questions, he is curious to know the sources from which these habits have been derived, that he may better understand their nature and tendency; as if well aware that the influence which sustains one form of government, and the impulse which presses forward the people to improvements, are both complex in their character and difficult of complete analysis. A South American who arrives in this country bringing the mind and education above supposed, becomes immediately possessed of this great idea; and when his knowledge of our idiom proves inadequate for the expression of his feelings, he is sometimes heard pronouncing his eulogiums in the harmonious and manly tones of his own language.

His face is not confined to any shade or hue.—It presents to us a variety of complexions, some darker, some paler, than the sun is wont to dye upon our cheeks. In their form and their features there is often a smaller proportion, and an expression of feebleness, as if nature had been struggling for generations against the enervating influence of an oppressive climate, and against a system of government still more oppressive, yet with a degree of success, or at least without having entirely yielded. Such an individual I can easily recall to memory. There were the remains of the bold Castilian contour in the face, and the sparks of genius among the ashes of a mind calcined by the long burning furnace of Spanish oppression. The eye was the only feature on which you could look without a mixture of compassion. That asked no pity. It shone bright as the sun in his climate, and sparkled from its deep recess as if the dark, overshadowing brows had protected it, and cherished it into more than native fulness and vigor. Like the plants that have rooted themselves in the depths of a tropical forest, on which the soil and the climate have operated with all their energy ; or like the gold vein in the mountain caverns, it shone with a richness and brilliancy to other regions unknown. Early in the first interview, his pallid hue prevented me from observing the muscular strength of his frame, which was in fact not below our own common standard ; and his earnestness gave to his tone and his attitude almost an appearance of one who argues for a cause he considers as already lost. But it was only because his subject, which was the liberty of his country, appeared to him far too great to be trusted to his energies. On the strength of its truth and justice he seemed rather to lean, than to offer it any unnecessary support ; and his manner, warm and animated on inferior topics, soon became kindled to enthusiasm. It was not without deep interest that any one could listen. A thought of the dark ages which had just passed over his ancestors, was succeeded by the reflection that his country was now revisited by day ; that Providence had begun to dispense to them a portion of those political, moral, and religious blessings which we have so long enjoyed, and which we hold so dear; and that the lot of one possessing so fine a mind was not, as in past days, to be crushed in the dust, and made to suffer in

proportion to its great and varied capacities. And
how doubly delightful is the thought, when we extend
our view to that world of gems, and consider that its
brilliancy is not to be longer confined to the pebbles of
the brook; that it will soon present treasures of more
intrinsic value than the gold in its mines; that in that
land of pearls, unheard of beauties shall be disclosed,
when education developes the traits of the female
character in the hearts of her daughters; that the
sun, which was formerly worshipped on some of her
shores, is but an emblem of the civil, intellectual and
moral light which will soon overspread her hills and
valleys; and that the streams which flow among the
richest productions that nature affords, will be visited
by science and virtue, even to their highest fountains.
If we so much rejoice when we hear of some victory
gained by civilization, on the rocky coasts of the northern seas, and the progress of improvement and happiness in regions where nature opposes all its obstacles,
it is reasonable to feel double gratification, when
national independence introduces refinements of every
description to a new continent, in which the soil, the
situation and the seasons combine to concentrate the
advantages of every clime: for the scene is not only
more extensive, but more prolific; and if such has
been its aspect when left waste and a desert, what will
it become when it shall blossom as the rose?

Burgoyne's Head Quarters.

RELICS OF THE REVOLUTION.

In pursuing the principal routes in the northern parts of the United States, the traveller's attention is frequently called to places which were rendered interesting by important events in the American Revolution. There are none of these more easy of access, and at the same time more worthy of remark on acacount of its history, than that elevated and commanding range of hills on the western bank of the Hudson, where the choice and powerful army of General Burgoyno was defeated by the American regular troops and militia, commanded by General Gates, in the year 1777. Since the field of Saratoga, or, more properly speaking, Bemis's Heights, has become well known to travellers and readers within a few years, it will not be necessary here to give a particular description of it. General Wilkinson's Memoirs contain the details of the two important days of September 19th and October 7th, with descriptions and maps of the ground; and Mr. Silliman's account of his observations made on the spot, a few years ago, which he gives in his " Short Tour to Quebec," will afford ample information to the visiter.

If the traveller approach the place from the south, he pursues the route taken by the American troops, who fled southward after evacuating Fort Ticonderoga, before the army of General Burgoyne. General Schuyler, who commanded the retreat in this direction, had thrown every possible impediment in the way of the invaders, and by energetic measures had prepared to meet the enemy with hopes of success, when he was most unreasonably superseded, and forced to resign the command to General Gates. The fate of the country, which was then menaced, might doubtless have been safely entrusted with either. By the route on which they had retreated the American troops were again led on, till they were stationed on the commanding range of Bemis's Heights, to dispute the road, that naturally lies along the narrow and level meadow extending from their feet to the river's bank.

If, on the contrary, the stranger's approach to the field be from the north, he takes the route of Burgoyne on his descent and his return ; and when the visiter to the field follows the path up the romantic and gloomy bank of the Cummingskill, he remembers with what different feelings the British General pursued the same way, before and after those sanguinary battles which decided the fate of his vaunted expedition.

The print at the head of this chapter is a sketch of Smith's little tavern, then Burgoyne's head-quarters, since moved a little from its place. The high ground in the rear was crowned with batteries, in one of which General Frazer was buried. In reviewing the field of Saratoga, the character of our revolutionary forefathers naturally presents itself to our minds in a forcible light. Although the appearance of the ground has been much changed by the removal of the forest trees, which then covered a great part of the heights, the form of the surface gives sufficient data to trace the most conspicuous scenes in the field of strife ; and many a visiter has in later years experienced excited feelings, on passing along the once-shaded course by which Morgan led on his riflemen at the beginning of the second contest, or trod the narrow space that once separated the two armies, over which the tumultuous waves of battle so many times flowed and ebbed, between the opposite skirts of the wood, which alternately afforded them shelter and a rallying place.

So long as the importance of the victory which was then achieved shall be appreciated, will the spot be visited with emotions of gratitude to Providence, and admiration for our forefathers. That race of men has now become few : decimated, over and over again, by the ravages of sixty years, their ranks, once so full and so irresistible, have been closed and closed again, to supply many a lamented vacancy ; and now present only a few greyheads and feeble frames, supported by tottering knees. It would be a subject worthy the ambition of our most accomplished writers, to portray the character of these old men, as it is presented in the different grades of society, on which they have shed so much dignity and honor ; to search out those who may be found in the retirement of rural life, objects of veneration to one generation after another : a sort of living monuments, exalted like columns of antiquity, and bearing the inscription of many a virtue.

As they came from the various grades and concerns of life to enter the field, and when they sheathed their swords returned to the retirement of their homes, they are now found in all the useful stations and employments which good old men can occupy ; and many a humble as well as many an honorable place is filled with double credit from their ranks. They are perhaps the only soldiers in the world who, after obtaining the most signal success, and while holding irresistible power in their hands, have suffered themselves to be disbanded, and cheerfully dispersed to their homes without reward, or even pay. They twice gained the country's independence by conquest, first from their enemies and then from themselves. Strange as the fact may appear to an European soldier, the explanation is perfectly understood here. They were themselves the country : the army of the revolution was never formed of a distinct body of men—the troops, the rulers and the subjects had all the same interests ; their dangers were the same, their hopes arose from the same sources ; they were in fact the same individuals, only differently arranged and acting in different capacities. The war was demanded by the people, each of whom knew that he must lend his individual exertions, and risk his own property and life to carry it on ; and many of them who thus aided in casting off the control of a foreign government. were afterwards called to assist in devising a new, to partake in administering it, and finally to live under it as subjects. The only object they declared in taking up arms, was the security of their rights : the only signal for them to resign them, was the evidence that they were established ; the only ground on which they now claim their victories is that those rights are effectually secured.

The men who came to fight for their country in the revolution, came like the streams which flow from the mountains, when their course is opposed by any obstacle. They combined all their power to remove the obstructions in their way ; and began to subside to their former level as soon as they were no longer there. However formidable their strength, however devastating their course while their force was exerted, they afterwards moved along in quietness and peace. Wherever they are found they still preserve characteristics which belong to no other individuals. Their youth and manhood were unlike those of any other men we ever saw or can see ; and their old age is such as will never be presented to the contemplation of our descendants.

The politicians of the present day, perhaps of all other personages, might visit some of these old men in their retirement with the greatest advantage. In their time there was no pecuniary reward to tempt men into prominent public posts. Those who look only for lucrative offices, would have found little temptation to seek the dangerous distinction of those days. Had things remained in that state until now, had the ways to distinction been, as at that time, still scattered with bullets instead of coins, how many *brilliant* talents might have been left in obscurity !

But how often is the revolutionary soldier passed

by, by those who do not appreciate, as a future age will do, their services and their characters! Under the slight which they receive from too many of their countrymen, however, they appear doubly estimable and reverend. There is always much to interest an observer among the useful employments in which they usually engage as long as their age will permit; and even in the harmless amusements with which they are sometimes obliged to beguile those latter days that early privations often mark with infirmity. The former scenes of their lives are ever uppermost in their thoughts; and time, which wears away the remembrance of those less important, seems to give to these a greater brightness. No wonder that the memory of the old man, tenacious of early scenes even to a proverb, should fix on them with interest, while we can overrate the trifles which occupy our time and attention. One will dwell on the impression produced on his youthful mind by the news of "the first shedding of blood;" and traces its influence on his subsequent life: it impelled him to Bunker Hill, or to the nearest battle-ground he could find, and enrolled him, without oath administered or proffered pay, among the soldiers of the revolution. One (and he has long been called an old officer,) speaks with enthusiasm of the character of his leader, Montgomery, and calls him his teacher in the school of true honor. Another, a man born poor and so to die, will give you a heart-rending picture of the carnage at Fort Clinton, and the agony of losing that post; while an individual of respectable family, an honorable post, and an independent estate, can describe, as he

has often described, the haste with which he obeyed the
summons to its relief, the anxiety with which he gazed
for the first sight of the fortress from the opposite
shore, and the distress which he felt on hearing the
cheers of the captors. One I could name, who from
the elevated hill on which his house is placed, can
point out the courses of the hostile expeditions which
devastated his village in the Revolution, and recount
the romantic history of some of the villagers who now
sleep in quietness in the grave yard, after all the
dangers and trials, the captures and exiles they had
passed through in the border war. Another, who was
called from a retreat far in the forest by the voice of
battle, now returns to his favourite scenes in the green
wood ; and with few early friends above the ground
but the old oaks and cedars, selects from them some
curiously bended staff to prop his tottering footsteps.
In his solitary walks at evening he often recalls the
cannon's roar, the trumpet's sound, and the feelings of
his youth.

There is not one of these, (for I can speak from observation,) who does not recover from the stoop of old
age, when the revolutionary times are spoken of ; or
when you tell them that by the token of their gray
hairs they ought to know something of the days when
the country was rescued from destruction by the hands
of a few hardy sons. We have never sufficiently
appreciated their characters ; we have not placed the
proper stress on those traits in which they differ from
European soldiers. It is, however, of the highest
importance that we should be strongly impressed with
the truth ; for so long as the subject is viewed in its

proper light, so far as the spirit and the men of our Revolution are revered as they deserve, so long will the United States be secure against themselves, which sound politicians regard as the greatest source of our danger.

Those who have an opportunity to see an European officer and one of our revolutionary period placed side by side, and to draw a comparison between their characters, will perceive a difference which cannot be reconciled, and which it would be almost impossible to describe in its full extent. One may be deeply versed in the science of war, and may consider himself as a sharer in the glories of some of the bloody campaigns which it has produced. He will square every thing according to his ideas of the honor of an army and the rights of a soldier. But he breathes a portion of the polluted atmosphere contaminated by standing armies. A man of just principles and pure mind associates with him only the recollections of the blood shed in vain, and worse than in vain, by Austrians and Italians, French and Spaniards, Swiss and Swiss —the devastation of neutral territories and frontier villages. He presents the aspect of a savage animal, armed by education with all the offensive and deadly weapons of art, which, when associated with his herd, and allowed undisputed range, has helped to spread death and desolation among the human race, and the habitations of man, with more rapidity and to a greater extent than the most violent tempest, the mightiest volcano, or the most desolating pestilence. Passions, never subjected to the control of humanity, religion, or justice, have stamped on his countenance on ex·

pression where cruelty, brutality, and perfidy can each
lay claim to a feature. There are glances which
are not to be found either in the wild wolf or the
tiger; for they would have shuddered at scenes which
he has both witnessed and perpetrated.

But turn to contemplate the calm and benignant
countenance of our revolutionary patriarch. There
you read something of the principles and the motives
he imbibed among the social circles where he spent
his childhood; the feelings which impelled him in the
scenes of his youth; and the sentiments of pleasure
and approbation with which he looks back upon them
in his old age.

Time, which tries all things, abundantly proves the
difference of these characters. While reduced and
disbanded armies have produced nearly all the dissentions and calamities which have befallen ancient and
modern nations, there has been no reason for restrain-
ing such men as those who filled the ranks in our revolution. Although the peace brought the dissolution
of their military existence, cut off even the prospect of
future pay, and gave them little hope of seeing past
promises fulfilled, there was one thing which they
found secured by it, and that was the thing of para-
mount value in their eyes—the country's independence.
This was the only reward which could ever have
satisfied them; is was the only object for which they
had taken up arms, and with that secured, they had
nothing to lose. Actuated by different motives, they
obeyed a different impulse from that which would have
operated upon other troops; and if we were wise
enough to appreciate the subject as it deserves, we

should make their character a more conspicuous object, when we speak of our national blessings; we should give them more room in the instructions of youth, and bring them out in a more prominent view for the contemplation of manhood. The recollection of the sincerity, the ingenuousness, the public spirit and honest, manly uprightness of our forefathers, ought to be borne into every department of our society. If our political men were actuated by them, how large a portion of our candidates would be rejected with scorn; how many of the plans of parties would fall with force on the heads of their projectors; and how many of their false professions would heap double disgrace on those who act in direct opposition to their words!

An old revolutionary soldier feels indignant at the party contentions of the present day; and it is only those of us who are conscious of being also out of the atmosphere of office-seekers, who can hear, with undisturbed consciences, of the defections which he charges upon this degenerate age. He learns of the tricks tried for the success of rival candidates, the projects for circumventing the checks and precautions of the constitution, with which so many of our politicians endeavour to compass the favourite wishes of those whose breath has created them; but to him they appear in their real deformity. Certain it is, that if the voices of our revolutionary old men were as prevalent as they were in more trying times, instead of being drowned by the clamours of millions of their juniors, they would be as firm and patriotic as ever, and the country would see many different names figuring in the list of its governors.

Is it not something like a reproach to the present age, that persons of this character find themselves obliged to confine their sympathy in past scenes entirely to themselves? The wants of the day, the concerns of a new and numerous society, afford us so many subjects of contemplation and concern, that few, very few, care for the trouble of learning the history of our war : as unknown, and as much overlooked by many, as if it were a matter of no concern to ourselves. Indeed, it may be seriously questioned, whether some foreign wars are not better and more extensively known in the United States, than that which gave us being as a nation. Besides, proud of the supposed superiority of our country and the age, (neither of which, perhaps, has yet been under consummate obligations to ourselves,) are we not ashamed to ask instruction of those old, gray-headed men, although we owe them all we have, and all our country possesses ?

Wo to the poor man who finds himself in a country village, or in the seclusion of any society where none of his comrades is to be found. Sympathy on the subject nearest his soul is denied him : the scenes of his youth pass silently and daily in review before his mind, but he finds no one to whom he can express the sentiments with which they fill him. He may recall scenes of which he can speak as an active agent ; and light may break in upon him concerning the designs of the commander-in-chief in this or that manœuvre which he had to perform ; or the overruling hand of Providence in the direction of a campaign, may be rendered more evident; or in his dealings with himself, his companions in arms, his company or regiment. But the world are busy about other things, and cannot spare the time or the labour, to listen to the plan of the battle, the state of the country, the hopes and fears, the dangers and exposures, the sufferings and the discouragements, which stamped the character of the period. For himself, why should he better accommodate his feelings to those of others, if they cannot, in some degree, share his own?

The Revolutionary old man is thus ranked with an isolated society, between the members of whom subsists a relation, which is not only acknowledged and felt by all, but is ever operative as a lively and prevailing passion: which grows more intense as the number of the survivors is diminished, and it is participated by a smaller and a smaller band. It is a subject worthy of attention, and which might well excite our interest, to observe how closely bound they are in the bonds of affection and fellowship, of mutual respect and esteem—the reverenced relics of an age which can never return—this society of benefactors, who deserve more gratitude than we can ever owe to others, or repay to them. There is not one of them who cannot name and number all his old brethren in the field within his district; and I should not desire a more grateful task, then to bear between them their messages of peace and remembrance. They send their greetings in a soldier's language, which may sound strange to our ears, but which carries an indescribable

welcome with it, and awakens in their honest hearts
recollections of more heroic, more active, more in-
spiriting days. And who would not wish to be present when two of them meet after a long absence, in
anticipation of another and a speedy interview, which
will be succeeded by no separation, if we could record the expressive eloquence of their language, with
every motion and every look ?

Those who never expect to meet in this world, will
often be found to entertain towards each other feelings of peculiar force, and of a peculiar character.
They are not such as can be described : the possessors rarely attempt to describe them. They are such
as nothing can produce but circumstances like· those
in which the individuals were once placed, and in
persons like themselves. Philosophers could not sa-
tisfactorily trace out the causes from which they had
their rise ; and, even if they could, language would
not be competent to communicate an idea of them.—
One of these old men will be heard inquiring of the
traveller if he has any where met with some old companion in arms :—" he must be an old man now, if
he is not already dead. He was my comrade or my
officer at York, or Morristown, or Bunker's Hill ; we
were together with Montgomery ; or he was drafted,
or volunteered with me for the sortie from Fort Stan-
wix. I should be glad to meet him again. I would
rather see him than any man living : he knew me
once, and I think cannot have forgotten me yet."—
Expressions like these, plain and brief as they usually
are, mean more than mere language seems to express : they have significations which we cannot

understand, and the speaker will not waste words on us.

They are men of whom we want to inquire much. We see the prosperous movements of the great machine of our government; but some of them could tells us of the difficulty of invention, the scarcity of the materials, the impediments to be encountered in prejudices, the boldness of hazarding the experiment. They speak with enthusiasm of the feelings which actuated—the motives which impelled them; and, at, the same time, with an almost superstitious awe do they look upon that period of their lives, when they observe the more than ample fulfilment of their hopes. They regard the end as one that no human eye could have foreseen, and therefore they are almost tempted to believe it was something more than human power that encouraged and upheld them. That period of their lives becomes to them one of deep interest, for they feel as if miracles had then been performed. They are ready to tell their children, "there were giants upon the earth in those days."

They look upon the country as in debt to them as the slave is indebted to his ransomer, the captive to his liberator, the blind to him that restores sight—and they say within themselves, I knew you when you were poor, and blind, and enslaved, and I freed and elevated you. So conscious do they feel of this fact, so clearly do they remember past scenes, so plain is the truth before their eyes, that they regard the United States as they lately were—few, weak, and defenceless colonies—so weak, that they supplicated even them for protection, with little prospect of being able to render

any reward. And they know in their hearts that no
hope of reward, no promise, ever persuaded them
even to buckle on the sword. It was the dictate of
their own judgment, backed, powerfully seconded by
their indignant feelings, which made them draw and
strike, conquer with, and then resign it into the hands
of the feeble state they had rescued. They are the
knights of our chivalry, and our country is the distressed fair they released from thrall. They feel like
a fond parent towards a child they have nourished in
its infantile and unprotected years; and when that
manhood comes, which is indebted to them ten times
over for its existence, not to mention its exaltation ;
and when pride and strength, of their bestowing, of
their gratuitous conferring, come in company with
neglect of benefactors, and contempt for their gray
hairs, who can lament, who can weep, who can peti-
tion ? You will hear them say—" We are sure of one
thing we have earned—we shall not be denied a grave
in the soil we have defended, and there we look for
rest, in our country's bosom." Our soil is not more
cold, not more niggardly of this world's wealth, than
some of the hearts among us, which beat with a life
of their preserving, and whose blood flows with the
liberty they gave. "We do not come like petitioners
to Congress," say they—" not like beggars—though
we have been called so in the city which bears the
name of a Leader, who would almost rise from his
ashes to repel the charge. We ask for a few of our
fellows, who are going to the grave, and have nothing
to hope for the children on whom they entailed poverty

by their sacrifices of possessions, and time, and health, and limbs to their country."

When conversing on subjects like these, the old men stand erect. Their tall and upright stature is like the stem of the mountain pine, which the lightning may rend but cannot bow, which ruin may prostrate, but cannot humble. Their forms were taught to stand erect by the very humiliation of their country; and they retain their elevation because they know in their hearts that in her days of darkness and despair they were her self-constituted deliverers. It is not mere nature that confers upon them the noble bearing which we admire; that bequeathes to them the front of the Roman champion, and lights up their sinking eye like the eagle's. When we come to stand where they now do, upon the brink of the tomb, we shall feel that age makes different forms and different features; and our children may exclaim for the glory departed. And what will be our glory, and what the vacancy we can leave! We have seen no such youth as these men; and such gray heads as theirs will not descend with us to the tomb. Well might we covet them, with all the decrepitude and all the neglect they have to encounter, if we might only bear with us the treasure they carry within their desolated breasts. That is the talisman which thus marvellously preserve their youth, and stamps on their features the winning, the irresistible traits of patriarchal majesty. I have seen one of their number wearying out the very sun in his daily race, in traversing, alone and unnoticed, the land he had helped to save; stooping to drink the unmingled spring, and reposing on the natural carpet of the

earth ; yet preserving his good conscience, and return-
ing blessing for scorn : for how could he complain of
the changes of Time, so long as it had thus fulfilled
his desires for his country, even to overflowing ? How
could he but thank that Providence which had disappointed even his youthful hopes, with an overwhelming accomplishment ?   How could he but smile, when
he had the consciousness, that she had been poor and
feeble as he was now, and he had consecrated to her
his strength, with the best of his days, and most ardent of his prayers ; when he now saw her enjoying
the fruits of his success, in ample, unhoped for, un-
thought of abundance and exaggeration ?

Such is the legacy left us by the past age, in the
examples of our forefathers ; and such are the lessons daily read to us, as they pass before our eyes,
and move along the path which conducts them to the
grave.   Italy has no memorials, no men like these.—
Greece may boast of her forms of marble, but let us
revere these heroic statues of flesh ; and if so much
as a single murmer should ever again be raised against
them in the Halls of Congress, let the thundering
voice of the nation visit the indignity on the head of
the offender !

AN INTERESTING STRANGER.

It may have happened to some recent travellers along our great routes, or passing through the crowded streets of our principal cities, to meet with such a stranger as I am about to describe. He belongs to a class entirely new in this country, and would at once strike an observer as an individual of a species hitherto unknown among us. Yet ignorant as we may be of his personal history, that of his native land is acknowledged to have been of the highest interest and importance, and is rising once more to view, soon to attract universal attention. However much we may feel at a loss to refer his aspect and his features, his manners and his mind, to any land within the compass of our observation, accompany him to a gallery of the arts, and perhaps you may trace a resemblance in the lineaments of those relics of antiquity that our artists copy with so much reverence. Among groupes of ancient statues he stands like one which has been singled out by Prometheus, differing from them but in life and motion ; and then he may be regarded as a fit emblem of his country, not essentially transformed, but only revived at the present day.

You may seek in vain to interpret his language by a recurrence to one of those most currently in use among us. His tongue is not that of the Italian or the German, the Gaul or the Iberian; and, though among the most refined of those multifarious combinations which form our own jargon, his ear may distinguish words which claim affinity with some of his own, it is only in the libraries of our most accomplished scholars, and in the works of the celebrated ancient writers, that he recognises the language he learnt on his mother's knee.

Such a stranger as this may perhaps pass in the crowd unknown, although not unnoticed; but he bears with him in his breast such thoughts as would enrich any mind. His lips are sealed to us, and his ignorance of our habits may cut him off from intimate intercourse with those around him: but the consciousness of what he has assisted to perform, keeps a warm glow in his exiled heart. He feels with rapture a living principle throbbing and reviving in his bosom, such as his fathers bore; and recognises the spirit of Greece. He loves to recall the impetuous pulse which gushed through his heart, when he took his stand at some of the gates of that renowned country, and aided to save her again from destruction, by such deeds as in ancient days were repaid by centuries of fame. The feelings of a patriot who has struggled, and not in vain, for his country, ever have been an abundant reward for his labours and his sufferings; but surely a magnanimous heart would set lightly by any trials which would identify him with the ancient heroes.

How is his mind employed—whither do his thoughts wander in his leisure moments? He inquires whether Greece is of less value than in the time of Xerxes, and whether the sacrifices and the exertions of soldiers who have now delivered her, are less great or meritorious than those of Leonidas. He reflects that what once rendered the salvation of his country valuable to the world, and glorious to those by whom it was accomplished, was not fully developed till subsequent ages; and that circumstances are in some respects more favorable now than formerly, for her rapid advance in intellectual greatness. All that lay in man has been performed by himself and his patriotic countrymen, and the future will show whether their exertions are to be crowned with as great results.

He looks around upon the prosperity of our young nation, and contemplates the operation of liberty here, with something like the feeling which we might suppose, in case the spirit of one of his ancestors could revisit the world. He refers every thing to its source; he traces to the example of his fathers many an impulse and many a principle which has guided us in the path of freedom and happiness. Among the sounds of our multifarious language, he recognises many an analogy with his own: but they are words which bear no sorrowful reference to the ages of darkness under which Europe suffered so long; they are not such as many a barbarous people and many a benighted age have engrafted by force on the dialects of Europe: but they are those which relate to the finest arts and the sublimest sciences; which are applied

10*

to the most beautiful objects of nature, and the most refined exercises of the mind. They are epithets and names for things which cannot exist in a depressed state of society, and which were disused in the dark ages, but on the improvement of the arts and sciences, the revival of knowledge, and the resuscitation of freedom, were sought again in the only language where they were to be found, and adopted, as that of the lost Pleiad would be, should it re-appear in the firmament.

He was one of those who raised the half-forgotten shout of liberty among the mountains of Greece, and taught the echoes again to repeat its once familiar name ; and it is with no small degree of pride that he surveys a country which the memory of his ancestors has successfully excited to establish national independence and personal freedom. Like the native of a tropical climate, ranging through our forests and gardens, where every thing he sees is admired in proportion as it approaches the splendour and luxuriance of his own more genial land ; and where the greenhouse dearly cherishes some plant that has been borne away from his country as a valued prize : the whole circle of our fine arts presents the Greek but humble imitations of the masterpieces of his countrymen. The scope of the ancient poets and philosophers is made the summit of perfection by our own ; and the higher he ranges among the upper spheres of our literature, the praise of his country is sung the more loudly in his ears.

On our part we regard the Grecian stranger with sentiments not less interesting, though perhaps more difficult to describe. He has come from a land traversed by the first apostles of our religion, from the scenes once illuminated by the golden candlesticks which its divine author planted, to diffuse his celestial light over the world, and where was early dispensed that truth which is of inexpressibly more value than all that the mere philosophy and learning of Greece could ever afford. Our old patriarchs would crowd around him with their bibles in their hands, to inquire for the relics of the ancient churches, to know whether they have survived the denunciations recorded in the apocalyptic visions. We would know whether there be not still some remains of the Corinthian christians to ponder over the epistles of St. Paul, once sent to their gates. The feelings of youth impel those who rise from the perusal of ancient history, to listen with fixed attention to every word he speaks of his country, of the scenes where great deeds were performed in former days, and of those which have been raised to dignity in later times, by what he and his countrymen have wrought. The student starts from his books at the sound of a language he had thought hushed forever in death ; and gazes at the personage who bears it upon his tongue with the familiarity of the nursery, as if he doubted whether he were not something else than flesh and blood.

But such is, notwithstanding, the fact : Greece has revived in our day, and with it perhaps may have commenced a new era, important at once to literature and politics, and interesting to men of taste and of philanthropy. Among the rekindling embers of ancient days, we begin to perceive what had passed

by unnoticed for ages : not only the unquestionable
relics of her language, but those of her genius, and
her national propensity for every thing great and bril.
liant.   The Greek informs us with exultation, that he
can now greet as brothers the freemen of all countries,
since the land of his ancestors has been rescued from
Turkish bondage ; and he longs to see assembled the
representatives of enlightened nations in that country,
to which they originally owe so much of their prosper.
ity and elevation.   He talks to us of the pleasure he
anticipates, in welcoming at some future time, on his
native soil, the sons of America—the land which has
offered him a solace in the time of darkness and exile.
And it is no unpleasing illusion to us, to picture the
scenes which some of our countrymen are destined
ere long to enjoy, in treading the mountains and tra.
versing the plains of Greece.   With what agreeable
sensations will they hereafter be reminded, by grateful
Greeks, of the exertions made on this side of the
Atlantic, few and feeble though they were, for the
succour of their distressed and heroic nation, in the
sufferings they had to endure in their desperate strug.
gle.

When the natural beauties of Grecian scenery,
mingled with the sublime features of her rocky
coasts and mountain ranges shall be known, through
the restoration of commerce to her ports ; and when
the traits of her literature, not less beautiful and not
less sublime, shall be more generally apprehended,
under a resuscitation of her language and of her early
writers, Greece will assume her appropriate place in
the heart of every man of taste and of learning :—

her ancient literary treasures will afford double attractions, and every department of science on which they have shed light will be reilluminated through all its ramifications.

It is not improbable that the influence of this important change in the affairs of the Archipelago, may be first rendered obvious in English poetry. There, it is certain, exists great room for reformation; and as both native Greeks and foreigners have already been inspired by the theme of liberty, it is to be hoped that they will not prove unmindful of the great models which it naturally brings up to memory. As every stream in that country has been long ago embodied in verse, and flowed on for centuries in numbers, no modern poet, methinks, would be bold enough to adopt a style at variance with that of the great masters who have rendered every subject imperishable. No hill or stream in that renowned land asks the modern poet for the aid of his lyre; and whoever is hardy enough to attempt a song in their praise, must remember he has a subject over the fame of which he can exercise no influence: one which has long been immortal.

Among those scenes, and in the places where the ancient Grecian poets once stood, could he descend to one of those feeble flights which have so often led to a near oblivion; or could he fail to be captivated with those strains which have not yet ceased to sound, and which will now waken in new vigor and sweetness? Will not the ancient taste be renewed, with all its natural force and beauty; and may not our poetry ere long feel its influence, and adopt something of its excellences? The poetry of the present day is unworthy of the state of improvement at which the civilized nations have in many other respects arrived, and of the boasts often made of a general progress in every thing. Perhaps some great genius may be drawn from obscurity, and tempted to under-take mighty things, when the models of antiquity are once more brought conspicuously before the world, and what is truly mighty in design and admirable in execution is once placed in its just contrast with the feeble, the timid, and the trifling productions of modern aspirants, or their perversions of verse, senti-ment, and truth. For it is not to be believed that every genius on which nature has bestowed superior powers, would consent to be fettered with the false rules of a preposterous taste ; and certain it is that those fetters have not yet been effectually broken. When the language of Homer and his long train of successive Grecian poets shall be resuscitated among us, and when the real and majestic sounds of their numbers shall strike upon modern ears, with something of their original harmony and strength, it cannot be that they will fail to attract the attention of the world, and that all harp strings will be so insensible as not to return a single responsive chord.

The Greek cannot mingle among us and not hear, with distress and indignation, some of the unjust reflections too often cast upon the character of his countrymen, on account of the dissentions that have occurred among their chiefs, and the examples of timi-dity or want of concert among the troops and the inhabitants on different occasions, magnified by their

avowed enemies, and backed by the prejudices entertained, by many of their secret ones. He protests
with vehemency, he argues with the eloquence of his
country, he appeals to scenes of bloody resistance
and cases of desperate determination, which he knows
in all their details, but with many of which we have
been left in ignorance, through the indirect communi-
cations we have thus far had with Greece. He re-
counts to us the deeds of the Suliots, at home and in
the various places to which their expatriation from
their native mountains dispersed them ; describes their
character, and traces their bright but brief career, to
the catastrophe of Missolonghi, where it may be said
to have terminated in the tomb. He speaks of Athens
and Argos, Tripolizza, Napoli, Malvoisia, Macrinovo,
and Navarino ; of Samos and Maina ; repeats the
names of Miaulis, Tombazis and Canaris ; and
estimates the rivers of Turkish blood which flowed
from the invaders, and gives a picture of the patriotic feelings which impelled some of the principal com-
manders, and many of the people themselves,—till
the tales of our revolution lose half their horror, and
much of their military importance. To show us that
the Greek, when exposed to an irresistible force, had
powerful motives to impel him to flight, he recalls the
tragedies enacted at Scio, Ipsara and Missolonghi ;
and enumerates a hundred names of towns, villages
and islands, lately smiling in unoffending peace, or
girt round with the few brave men who risked their all
for liberty, now ruinous, desert and silent : regions
over which the scourge of the false prophet has passed,
and with horrors too great for man to listen to,

much more for tender females and babes to endure,
wasted, crushed and ravaged, leaving none to be in-
jured by the enemy, or by the hunger, nakedness and
agony which followed in his train. Of these horrors
says the stranger, an American cannot, without an
exertion of his imagination, form even a distant idea.
Look at the little children who have at different periods of the war sought a refuge in your distant land.
Some of them you have loved for their helpless and
friendless condition, and admired for the bright talents
they have shown, in their animated countenances and
their active minds. Such are the orphans which have
been made by the Turks; and thousands of such are
now scattered over the most humane regions of Europe,
while greater multitudes are laboring and lamenting
in captivity, among their barbarian masters. Their
mothers, and their sisters, where are they? When
we reflect on the fate of many of them who are now
alive, it is a relief to think how many fell in the desolation of Scio, and we almost regret that more had
not been immolated at Missolonghi. Scenes like
those, where hundreds destroyed themselves, afford a
terrible but a just comment on the character of our
enemies. When delicate women and tender children
coolly and deliberately walk from the verge of a rock,
or the walls of a fortress, or dispute for the spot over
the centre of a mine, dissatisfied with every thing but
certain death, and envying their companions if they
obtain a place rather more fatal than themselves,
there must be some horrible terror that operates upon
their minds. Yet such has been the plain, unvarnish-
ed truth, times unrecorded, during the late war in

Greece. Imagine how such a thing would appear to your eyes; for when one has witnessed it he is convinced that feelings are excited difficult to be conceived by those who have not. Imagine one of the most delicately educated of your countrywomen, with one of the most interesting and affectionate children: what would be your feelings to see her, in the frenzy of dread, stab her child and plunge headlong into the sea or upon the rocks? And yet such things have been familiar to us; nor these alone—but, what was more dreadful still, the sight of our dwellings destroyed, during our absence in war, by barbarians who had torn away alive our mothers, sisters and wives. Tales of such events would sometimes reach the ears of a soldier while under arms in sight of the foe: the first impulse would dispose him to fly for home; and this was repeatedly done, even when the distance was so great as to render assistance hopeless, in spite of the intreaties, arguments and threats of their officers. The second impulse turned them in the opposite direction: to wreak a vengeance which knew no adequate language, and no satisfactory limit, on the wretches who had brought such intolerable woes on the Greeks. Many a bloody action has owed its impulse, if not its termination, to the untameable spirit thus aroused: where of hundreds of Turks who started at the first war cry, not one survived to hear the closing shout of victory. The memory of such scenes, or the thought of friends, parents, children and wives, who have been the victims of them, has often visited the soldier in his wakeful nights, and melted him to tears on his sentry post: it has cast a

11

melancholy aspect over the fairest of our landscapes, and made many a day to rise in sorrow and set in weeping. Such reflections have stimulated us to climb many a rude mountain, to perform many an incredible march, to endure hunger and weariness, watchings and wounds, as long as nature would allow us to endure. They made our people resolve to perish by any death, rather than again submit; and added if possible, to the resolution and the devotion of the Hetarists themselves, whose oath bound them never to know a resting-place till Greece should be free.

Still the Greeks are charged with the destitution of national feelings, and of being incapable of acting in concert by their party antipathies. But recurring again to the favorite period of ancient history, when the most pure patriotism is thought to have prevailed: in the last Persian invasion, the Greek auxiliaries marched against their country by thousands; in the battle of Platæa not less than fifty thousand were engaged against their brethren. Thermopylæ itself came well near not being immortalized; for the few Spartans who there surrendered their lives, were the only Greeks who had the spirit to make such a sacrifice. When the history of Modern Greece is once written as it deserves, it will be found that we have made numerous Thermopylæs, and have not been destitute of Spartans. On the sea, the more congenial element of the Greek at the opening of the war, deeds of individual prowess have been exhibited which were never surpassed. The immeasurable disparity of our forces, in point of the number and size of vessels, and the want of a general authority to conduct a combined operation, permitted no engagements like that of Salamis, as the merchant brigs of which the squadrons were composed were all private property : but the immense Turkish hulks, from time to time driven on shore and sunken by our fire-ships, would almost have contained the flotilla of Xerxes, numerous as were the gallies of which it consisted. One of the most admired periods of the history of the ancient Athenians, and that in which their patriotism is considered to have risen to its highest pitch, was the time when the Peloponnesians proposed to withdraw their frontier fortresses to the Peninsula of Corinth, leaving Attica to the possession of the enemy. The Athenians, at that time, solemnly determined thenceforward to make their ships their country, and to seek in some distant land a new home for themselves and their families. Such a plan, merely proposed by them, was actually put in practice by the Ipsariots ; who, when their little island was ravaged by a barbarous enemy, after all the resistance in their power had been made, betook themselves to the most destructive of the elements, and thus preserved that liberty which few others would not have preferred to surrender.— The Hydriots more than once contemplated such a step, and needed not the spirit to take it. The fortifications of their little rocky island, (which might well forego all celebrity in ancient times to take the conspicuous stand it has occupied in modern days,) were lately prepared for a forlorn hope, by hands which would have done desperate things in its defence ; and if Providence had not prepared for a more merciful interposition for Greece than most of her well-wishers

hoped for, a scene as terrible as the war had produced
might perhaps have been enacted there. But even
in the worst event the Greek race and the Greek spirit
would not have been exterminated: the fleet would
have spread its sails, and perhaps the remnant of that
nation would have found an asylum on this side of
the Atlantic."

It is natural for every one who has been taught to
pronounce with reverence the language spoken by
the great men of ancient Greece, and that in which
a portion of the Holy Scriptures was written by the
Evangelists, to ask with some solicitude whether there
be any possibility that it may be ever recovered.—
The native replies, much to the astonishment of his
hearers, that no recovery is necessary : that the iden-
tical language of ancient times is spoken now, with
no essential alteration. But how, we inquire, more
naturally than judiciously, how can it have been preserved through so many centuries, and under so many
disadvantages ?—and how can a Greek be a competent
judge of that ancient language, which, we have been
taught to believe, is nowhere found but in the ancient
writers, and to which the only approach lies through
the universities of Europe and America? Who can
be competent to pass an opinion concerning it, but
those who have formed an acquaintance with it in this
manner? The stranger answers us with a smile, that
the civilized world have not been aware how much
the scriptures have done to preserve the language of
Greece, nor with what facility, as well as delight, a
native of that country may understand many of the
ancient writers. "We have had a few schools," he

remarks, " of which you have been ignorant ; and the *rhapsodies* of Homer have been repeated in them by rote as exercises for juvenile rewards. Xenophon has been read by persons educated only in the rudiments of knowledge, and that too with a pronunciation that would have been much more intelligible to our renowned ancestors than to yourselves. The polished classes of society use a language which approaches that of the early times ; and as the latter is always the standard, a few years of liberty and peace, of plenty and refinement, would probably restore our style almost to the point from which it has descended. The changes it has undergone are surprisingly few—our isolated situation, a respect for our origin, and the presence of an unalterable standard hedging out almost every great innovation ; and at this day, Greeks meet and readily converse, from the most remote islands and the most secluded mountains of the North. the East, and the Morea, some of whom were but a short time since ignorant of each other's existence, while others were acquainted but to hate and to fight. The sounds of the letters of Cadmus are the same in all ; for the few and slight variations are not worthy of a general notice ; and the changes in construction, which some have called radical changes, find authorities, more or less sufficient, in the common Greek writers."

But, as on subjects of which we have every thing to learn, and at the same time require to be convinced against our prejudices, the adept in ancient Greek feels a repugnance to concede that the language he has regarded with such distant awe and almost super.

11*

stitious reverence, has been used by this stranger in
the common concerns of life. That it may be acquired,
in modern times, in the nursery, seems to depreciate
the value of our studious hours, and pride whispers to
us of the loss of much time, and of irksome labor devoted to our accidents, our articles, and our synopsis.
One of our scholars starts back also at the confused
and intricate appearance of a modern Greek manu-
script, and is ready to pronounce its aspect alone a
sufficient proof of the entire corruption of the language. " Here," he exclaims in triumph, " is the
penmanship of our scholars, which corresponds precisely with the ancient text !"

" Yes," replies the Greek, " and it corresponds also
with the hand-writing of our children and our educated men, because it is a copy of the same model.
You imitate the stiff printed text ; they copy, perhaps,
the ancient inscriptions on our monuments of stone.
We, however, use the *written letters* of Greece when
we write ; and a little practice would show you that
it is convenient and proper.   The time cannot be far
distant when the prejudice will be removed which
prevents your learned men from adopting this style of
writing, and of renouncing the ridiculous system of
pronunciation, which is of far greater consequence.
It cannot be long before your scholars will perceive
the reasonableness of adopting our pronunciation.—
A little reflection will show them the conclusiveness
of our arguments, and induce them to reject the fashion
introduced by a modern without any solid grounds."—
To them we have a right to look for this important
step : but we may rest assured, that if they do not

lead the way, the change will be shortly effected through the intimate intercourse which is likely soon to be established between the United States and Greece. Americans need but to visit our country, or to wait until our enterprising seamen shall furl their sails on this side of the Atlantic, to hear the ancient Greek tongue, preserved as it has been for centuries, without any irreclaimable degeneracy. The ages that have passed in such gloom over my native land, have seen the people retire to the fastnesses of the mountains, to which those who were able retreated, with their simple habits of life, their spirit of liberty, their traditions of departed greatness, and the religion and language of their ancestors. Those who could not avoid a more near approach to their conquerors, have still been able, in a good measure, to keep the sacred repository in their breasts; and the Greek, to this day, is found, in many respects, as distinct from the Turks, as if they had never come into contact. When the besiegers of Missolonghi railed at the slight breastworks of that fortress, the defenders replied—"The walls of Missolonghi are our breasts;" and they had been for centuries the effectual barriers against all that the detested Mussulmen brought in their train, except only the sword. When we lately determined on resistance to that, we had but to recur to our history for examples, as we did to the lips of our heroes for words to express every newly roused feeling of our hearts, and even the names of some of the weapons which we grasped at for vengeance. Thermopylæ and Thebes, Athens and Corinth, Argos and Mantinæa, heard the watch-words of ancient times revived, and passing from mouth to mouth along our lines ; and when we shouted victory, the echoes re. plied in once familiar terms."

With such remarks as these the modern Greek of education and feeling will entertain and instruct us, not to say, teach and chide. No wonder he should meet with those who lend attention. But among all he finds none who are more sincere or more lively in their expressions of interest in the sufferings of his countrymen, than the old men of our revolution. To many of them, the condition of Greece during the war presented an affecting appeal, on strong and various grounds. Those who had experienced the alarm and the distresses of the period when our own country was in extremity, best knew how to sympathise in such a case ; and they acknowledged, with shuddering, that the barbarities perpetrated by the Mussulmen far, far surpassed even what they had ever suffered or even apprehended. Refined as were many of our officers, and many of our soldiers, by a polished education, and an attachment to the principles of the gospel, they have been able to appreciate the classical associations of that land of fame, so justly delightful to real taste, while they have felt the ardent affection of Christians towards the soil so early favoured by the light of religion. The good tidings which we occasionally received from Greece, during her desperate struggle, brought disinterested joy to the dwellings of all these old men, and excited them to thanksgiving : and when, as was too often the case, details of massacres and horrors more terrible than death were received, they would bend their faces to the ground, as

they once did at the news from Quebec and Ticonderoga; and declared what they would have done in
their youth.

Some would have us undervalue the resolution, endurance and perseverance with which the Greek revolution was carried on, and the desperate, the indo-
mitable spirit by which alone it was rendered successful. So it did lately appear to our cool calculators,
and so it may appear to those who retain the blame-
able indifference lately so fashionable. But so it will
not seem to such of our countrymen as hereafter shall
visit the Archipelago, when they begin to ask for the
old bearings of the Sunium Cape, and follow the
wake of the Athenian navies into the port of Piræus;
when they joyfully tread the strand of Attica, renew
the ancient sites marked by the ruins of centuries, and
hail the majestic hills of Athens as they rise to view
before them. Their sentiments will not be of the
cold and hesitating kind, when they come to converse
in person with the liberators of Greece, and partake
with them of the rich intellectual feast which their
history offers; or to indulge with them in the delightful anticipation with which every philanthropist now
turns to their country.

A VISIT TO THE SENECA CHIEF RED-JACKET.

How deeply it is to be regretted, that the Indian character, which was marked by so many excellencies in its original state, should have deteriorated and been destroyed in proportion as it has been influenced by the approach of civilized men. No people, with whose history we have any acquaintance, ever possessed more hardihood or perseverance; greater attachment to personal freedom; superior aptitude and strength of mind—and none ever excited greater expectations by their capacity for improvement. Qualities less admirable than theirs, and less decidedly marked, have in other countries laid the foundation for the most enlightened and most powerful nations that ever existed. The native sagacity of the Indian, if employed on the sciences, might ere this have greatly assisted their progress; his generous, manly, and noble feelings, if exhibited in a civilized cabinet, might have produced a sensible effect on the aspect of politics: and if all the admirable traits of charac-

ter they possessed, instead of being **crushed in the
dust,** could have been encouraged by appropriate
motives, cherished by occupation, and subjected to
the influence of christianity, how different a spec-
tacle might now have been presented, and how different might have been the prospects of the Indian
race! The exertions which were made for their
benefit, on different plans and at different periods,
although directed by humanity, have proved unavail-
ing, except in very partial degrees, and to a very
limited extent ; and now, so ignorant do our government appear of the nature of man, and so predomi-
nant has become the influence of an unprincipled
self-interest among the American people, that the
prevailing cry is against their capacity for improvement, while the authorities of the United States, and
some of the members of the Union, at the same moment, are urging their forcible removal out of our
territory, because some of them have already improved too much.

If an unjust measure like this should be adopted
towards them, and banishment from their rightful possessions be added to the other crimes which white
men have perpetrated against them, how long may we
expect to hold the soil so unrighteously obtained ; or
to enjoy freedom, peace and happiness in regions we
desolate by force?

The solitude, wildness, and silence of the fores
encouraged such reflections, as I pursued my way
along the devious and almost undistinguishable path
which conducted me, with many windings, towards the
habitation of a chief of the Senecas. The forest—a

portion of that " great and howling wilderness," which
on the arrival of our ancestors, extended from the
Atlantic to the Pacific, and from the Gulf of Mexico
to the northern boundary of vegetation—was restricted within narrow boundaries a few miles in circuit : a
little remnant of that new continent in which our
forefathers found so many friends. The flourishing
village I had just left, rising on the shore of the lake,
and full of activity and life, was but a specimen of
the scenes which enterprise had extended in all directions to very distant limits, up to this circumscribed barrier. Here was a portion of the American soil as it lay before it was tutored by cultivation ; here alone, for miles beyond miles, the plough
had never entered, and the roots of the original forest
trees had never been disturbed. On all sides around
this secluded spot, every thing was full of activity and
thrift, and every one was looking on the future with
gay and brilliant anticipations. Here, every thing in
retrospect was grand and impressive : but all the
future was sad and mournful. The simple race,
whose remnants I was about to see, had raised no monuments of brass or stone to commemorate their departed greatness ; but the slow stream of the Buffalo
seemed overcharged with the tales of past ages, like
a tongue oppressed into silence by things too great for
utterance ; and the venerable oaks which grew on its
banks, I knew had been contemporaries of events they
could not record, and the witness of which was to
perish with them. The stillness of the forest reminded me of the closed lips of their masters ; who,
having no other depository for their pride, and no

other way to triumph over their oppressors, will not deign to communicate one word of their traditions, but prefer to drown them in their breasts, as the Incas sunk in their lakes the gold and the gems which they knew were objects of covetousness to their Spanish persecutors. The surrounding scenery naturally awakened again recollections of those traces of former greatness which are preserved in some of the characteristics of the Indian, and in the structure of his singular language—those things which have led the learned investigators of Europe to attribute to them a lofty, though a dark and undiscoverable origin. A people, who, even in their greatest degradation, can meet misfortune with a proud and uncomplaining silence, who can not only endure the pangs of bodily torture with stoicism for a few hours, but injustice, oppression, want, and contumely from the cradle to the grave, from those who owe them the soil they subsist upon, the air they breathe, and the superfluous wealth they so inhumanly refuse to share with them even in their greatest need, such a people must have descended from a stock unaccustomed to bend—the noblest growth of the forest. The remarkable character of their language, a very slight knowledge of which has excited the admiration and the highest eulogiums of learned philologists, must it not, at some period, have given utterance to conceptions of corresponding superiority and refinement?

The aspect of nature around me was as simple as it would have been if human invention had never been cultivated elsewhere ; and the men I was shortly to see were not those who sought or obtained distinction by the unmanly arts by which it is often attained in civilized life. They belonged to a race who had contested, not with chicanery, duplicity, and sophistry, but with wild men, wild beasts, the sun, the wind, and the storm. They were mighty men, men of renown; who had "waxed valiant in fight, and turned to flight the armies of the valiant." Here, on this soil, our ancestors had sought and even supplicated their assistance; for the Senecas, even as our own unwilling history acknowledges, were once almost arbiters of our destiny. Here the distinction is now, as it always has been, in being bold, active, and strong—goodly men, higher than all the people, have ranged these forests, and pursued shady paths, long since bared by our encroachments, with no opponents, because they were their own sufficient champions.

In a state of society like this, there always have been attractions to one disgusted by the injustice, the selfishness, the unrighteous exercise of ill-gotten power by which the eyes of man in the civilized state are continually assailed. Even the good man, the christian, might in some cases become so weary of looking on the false principles and practices which are in vogue and in operation around him, as to wish for the return of the simple virtues and the simple days of the patriarchs. Instances have never been wanting, since the contrast was first presented between these two states, where men of warm feelings have given the preference, on some accounts, to the life of the savage. Individuals who have become disgusted at the chicanery of knaves and the selfishness of commercial transactions; who have witnessed scenes

where gold has severed very friends, and known the
bolts and gratings through which the too sanguine
though honest debtor has sometimes to look out upon
his cruel but licensed oppressor; instances have not
been wanting of such persons turning a more apolo-
getic eye on the faults of the Indians, and doing more
justice to their virtues. Among them flattery does not
blandish crimes into excellencies; wealth does not
purchase a right to depress those whom nature or
goodness has exalted. Stepping into this shady
grove, I have withdrawn myself from the territory of
those habits and influences among which only I have
heretofore seen men. I look in vain for costly edifices, which nourish diseases of the mind and of the
body, while they serve as memorials to the poor of
the power of that great arbiter, gold. I look in vain
for prosperous indolence, for luxurious ease: the
graces of a generous heart and a noble mind, a powerful arm and an agile foot, are the qualities which
secure distinction here. In regions like this, before
the Indians had become contaminated by civilized
vices, such was the state of things which our ancestors
found, whenever they stepped into the shade of the
forest; and such might we still have found to this
day, had not our communication corrupted them. The
wrecks we see are ours; the few remains of what is
virtuous, valuable, and admirable, are their own, and
have survived in spite of us. These remains it is
still interesting to see; and it is strange that we have
so much obtuseness of feeling, and so much coarse-
ness of taste, as to pass them by unnoticed and unen-
joyed. The firm and impartial administration of jus-

tice under their simple laws, if brought into contrast
with cases which we sometimes witness in civilized
courts; and the strong bonds of gratitude, respect,
and patriotism which generally attach them to their
nations and tribes, even though extermination itself
strives to break them, might make a white man ashamed
of the party-spirit and selfish jealousies by which our
states, cities, and neighbourhoods are so often divided.
Sentiments of international faith are also to be found,
even to the present day, among these simple people,
which have been handed down by the traditions of
generations, and preserved inviolable for centuries,
oftentimes at no small sacrifice of convenience and
property.

Reflections like these are naturally suggested in
the solitude and silence of one of our Indian reser-
vations; and we cannot wonder that individuals were
formerly captivated by the simple virtues of such a society, and for them renounced, at least for a time, the
corrupt scenes of civilization. In the eyes of cool reflection, the revered turf over a warrior's grave, is
incomparably preferable to the false epitaph on a
polished monument; and the insincerity of fashionable language sinks into merited contempt, when compared with the few and direct words of the Indian,
almost incapable of perversion or duplicity. Here are
no irksome barriers, erected by wealthy and over-
bearing landlords, such as restrict within narrow
limits the steps of man in our territory; and here are
none of those subtleties of law by which the consci-
ously innocent are made to bear imputations of crime.
Impediments like these, though imposed by us to re-

strain the bad, often prove injurious and sometimes
fatal to the good.   Here the only human law is that
engraven on the conscience, and enforced by custom;
and the unfortunate and friendless may wander where
he will, without encroaching on the possessions of the
mercenary or low-minded; with the tallest oaks and
cedars for his shade, the purest streams for his drink,
the birds for his musicians, the recesses of the forest
for his retreat, the most secluded cavern for his place
of repose, and the calmness and harmony of nature
around to spread a placid peace over his slumbers.—
Here, without interruption, he may listen to the voice
which in these solitudes, is perpetually proclaiming,
like the Mahomedan crier, " there is no God but God."
He may pluck at freedom the ripest fruit and the
fairest flower; the largest fowl, the finest trout, the
swiftest deer is his which his weapons can overtake
or his art beguile.   The animals which course through
the woods are forbidden him by no law, "domitæ na-
turæ," for through all these wilds nature has never
been subjected to the hard conditions of human bondage; and the laws of the forest leave every thing as
free as the wind, that can survive or avoid the point of
the arrow.

Reflections like these, I know not how long continued, were interrupted by the sudden appearance of
a group of wild beings on a morning excursion for
game, with their long white blankets fastened at their
necks and flowing behind in the air as they ran.   One
was prying through the low branches of a tree, with
an eye, a step, and a ready finger which spoke whole
pages of archery.   Another drew an arrow to his ear,

and throwing off his loose blanket, dashed through a
thicket for his prey, almost at its heels. Three or four
were standing in consultation on a bright margin of
green grass, which skirted the edge of the neighbouring grove, and in their graceful forms and fine attitudes, seemed a group of the ancient woodgods.—
The expressions of their faces were much stronger
than those of common white men, as the features
of the Indians are generally larger, and drawn with
more boldness. From this remark however should
be excepted the eyes, which being of a deep black,
small, and much sunken, give them something of the
aspect of blindness near at hand, though at a distance
this peculiarity is not at first observed. Their dark
complexions were betrayed on their breasts, which
looked like those of bronze statues, while their gay
and tasteful savage ornaments were placed in a kind
of harmony with the yellow tinge of the walnut
leaves, the crimson of the maple, and the scarlet
vines that were seen clinging to the wasted trunks of
former centuries : for the season had blasted the
forest, as fortune had ruined the Indian race. These
were the looks of the Indians, these their habits, this
their abode ; in such simplicity, and often in such
security and innocence did they live, while the other
quarters of the world were deluged in blood, quite
as much as illuminated and refined by the arts
and sciences. The contest which commenced when
those arts were brought into collision with the simple
means in possession of the natives of these forests,
seems too unequal to have allowed of hope. Yet
with such feeble weapons did they persevere in their

resistance ; while the shades of their forest often
screened from sight their manly breasts which trusted
to no other shield. The echoes then lent their voices
to celebrate their victories, and replied to their shouts.
But the words of their singular language have almost
ceased to be heard throughout the whole extent of
their country ; and into oblivion they will shortly descend, with the many evidences they afford of 'a
lofty origin, and all those strains of native beauty and
sublimity which tradition herself will soon forget.—
Those bursts of natural poetry that no written record
has ever known, which any civilized nation of Europe
would be proud to quote as the productions of their
early ages, and which would be considered by the
learned as decisive proofs of native genius—all are
soon to be lost with the fleeting breath to which alone
they have ever been entrusted. The germs of national
greatness are thus sometimes blighted in the seed ; while
plants of less elevated origin take root and overspread
a continent and last through ages. Whoever views
this subject in such a light, will listen to the sound of
the Indian tongue with a melancholy interest. We
have not the advantage, indeed, of viewing the heroic
age of the Indian, through a long vista of past generations, and through the somewhat deceptive representations of polished writers ; but we have the sorrowful task of contemplating an early death, and a
rich but blasted prospect. A young pine of the forest
dissevered from its trunk, or a pure fountain which
after a short course is dashed over a precipice, is not
an unapt metaphor to represent such a placid course
conducting to so mournful an end.

My path grew more and more indistinct, until its
windings were only intimated by the smoothness of
the turf, which often left me in perplexity, till it at
last brought me to the view of the abode of the chief.
He had penetrated, like a wild beast, into the deepest
recesses of the forest, almost beyond the power of a
white man to trace him. A wild beast! but I found
him in a calm, contemplative mood, and surrounded
by a cheerful family. Old and young, collected
about the door of the log hut, where he was seated,
seemed to regard him with affection; and an infant
which one of the females held in her arms, received
his caresses with smiles. It was a striking scene—
a chief! Yet some of his inferiors who cultivate the
soil in other parts of the Seneca lands, had abundant
fields and well-filled store-houses, while he was poor,
but bore his privations with apparent equanimity. If
he had power, he did not exert it : if he had passions,
they were quiescent : if he had suffered injuries, they
were buried in his breast. His people had endured
sore and irreparable wrongs : it seemed to me that
their hopeless degradation and his own was uppermost in his thoughts, and was the habitual subject of
his meditations. His looks, his motions, his attitudes,
had that cast of superiority, which convinced me that,
whether justly or not, he considered no man his superior in understanding. His eye was not accustomed
to look abroad for the opinions of others ; and his lips,
which were once those of an accomplished savage
orator, refused alike to utter any language but that of
the Senecas, and any other sentiments than his own.
He appeared to regard himself as the only one of

his nation who retained the feelings and opinions of
his ancestors, and to pride himself in preserving them.
However others might be disposed to forget and for.
give injuries, as far as in him lay they were to be
perpetuated.   Biting sarcasms on the inconsistency
and perfidy of white men were ready on his tongue,
and were pronounced with that unmoved look and
voice which showed that he contemned as well as ab-
horred our race.   The wound inflicted on his heart
was still fresh and rankling ; yet his brow was clear
and his words were few.   Civilization had rolled by
him, with its flood of refinement, wealth, and happiness, but he had clung to his native poverty without
stooping to taste of the draught, because it was proffered by a whiteman.   A thousand miles towards the
West had it fertilized the wilderness : but not a trace
of its course was to be seen around him.   What bitterness must keep the door of such a heart ! and
how do our guilty consciences enhance the meaning
of his reproaches and his looks !

The forest still grew inviolate around him, and the
branches of the unpruned vine bent gracefully down
from the verge of the maple grove, to proffer its clus-
ters, and to extend its shade, to cheer the abode of
its preserver, and to add its little solace to the last
friend of the forest.   The sportive dwellers of the
wood, the squirrel and the singing bird, might well
make the spot their favorite resort, and gambol in
security before the door of the chief.   His fall might
be the signal for the axe to begin its work of devastation ; and the peacefulness that reigned around
might soon be dispelled for ever.   If there were any

birds or beasts of prey, they avoided his presence, and shrunk from his path ; and well might they enter- tain an hereditary dread of such as he. As he sat meditating, he explored the shades around with an eye that could pierce like an arrow into ages that are past, and look alike on disappointment and prosperity. The eye of an Indian seems almost to defy the power of circumstances and time, of nature and of man, to change its expression. It is, however, subject to change, though only a close observer can discover it : it expands so little and is shaded so much. With the same glance does he look on the height of dominion and the depth of degradation. That is the eye with which the first sail was studied as it approached the American coasts, bringing with it the leprous plague of white men ; so Uncas looked on Miantonimoh—so Miantonimoh returned the look of Uncas.

This is what remains of the once powerful, rich, and persuasive orator of the Senecas. This is the aspect in which he may be viewed by those who wish to put his vices and his degradation out of the range of observation. But he in fact presents a specimen of the degraded Indian character and Indian habits. against which the influence of civilization has been exerted for two hundred years, and the ruin of which we have effected. The delirious draught, which we have always first extended to that race, he has ac- cepted, and quaffed to the dregs : and now, in the prostration of his once noble powers of mind, and in the desperation to which the destruction of his people and himself has brought him, he madly insists on re- jecting the only remaining hope that is offered in this

world and the next. Christianity, so often disgraced in
his eyes by our individual and national policy towards
the Indians, he regards as the religion of traitors and
oppressors ; and he would have his people exclude the
very sound of the gospel. In the small domain where he
presides, the Christian shudders to think that he is in a
Pagan land ; and he is not happy until he enters those
tracts where the Senecas have admitted improvements,
and where some of their aged chiefs have bowed to the
supremacy of divine truth. They have felt their hearts
assailed at a quarter where the Indian is apt to think
he is not exposed to an attack, by the melting tones of
the Gospel ; and these, when brought home to their
minds, were so plain, so unanswerable, and conveyed
in language so like in simplicity to their own, that
they could not withstand them. Like those of their
race who once listened to Elliott and Brainerd, they
were made captives to the truth before they ever
thought of resistance; and the fervor with which Indians embrace its sublime and delightful doctrines, is
such as might be expected from men of their strong
and ardent feelings.

Among such individuals the man of piety, and even
of benevolence alone, finds what is necessary to en-
courage hopes which an interview with such as Red
Jacket may have banished from his mind. When he
sees the Indian husbandmen submitting to that patient
daily labor which their ancestors despised, and finds
that they begin to appreciate the blessings of civilization ; that they can reject the poisonous draught
which has sent so many of their race to the tomb, and
endeavour to introduce the knowledge of letters and

of the gospel, with those useful arts and those industrious and virtuous habits to which the white men have
owed their prosperity and happiness, then the stranger
begins to look to futurity with some agreeable anticipations for this despised, abused, but not quite ruined
people.

While we contemplate only their misery and degradation, we are disposed to inquire—What national
sin has brought a curse upon their heads? Why does
success for ever refuse to attend their paths? Why
does evil fortune persist in thwarting every project
intended for their good? What power diverts every
blessing designed for an Indian head, yet preserves
so tenaciously the wrecks of all their greatness? By
what tenure, amid their trials, do they retain an all-
enduring mind? Who is it that upholds their trampled
hearts, and teaches them to face misfortune with a
spirit unsubdued and an eye unquelled? But when
we see the evidences which have been repeatedly
presented to us, of the capacity of the Indian to improve in knowledge, character, and condition; when
we recall the simple tales of our early missionaries,
of their sincerity in embracing the doctrines of the
gospel; and contemplate the arts and improvements
which several nations of them have adopted, with the
interesting situation of the Cherokees, who have
formed a written constitution; we are ready to exclaim—There is something yet in store for them; a
step which descends so majestically to the shore, the
foot that is planted so firmly—so lordly on the brink,
is not destined to go down to annihilation. The waves
which roll before them, are already dyed with the

blood of their predecessors, whose **wrongs and whose**
sufferings no tongue can tell : but we wait, **expecting**
to see the sea divide, and open some path for their sal.
vation. To many of the individuals, however, we
can point, and say they are marked out for destruction.

This I felt while in the presence of the lonely chief
I had sought out in his retreat. The cloud which
hangs so dark over his race will burst at least upon
his head—for him destruction is inevitable. This he
knows, and he also knows there is but one mode of
escape, yet he rejects it, and would have his people
reject it. Fortunately not a few of them are sagacious
enough to adopt it ; and the traveller who enters
their churches and school-houses, or looks upon
them and their families in his tour, will fancy that he
finds among their little children those who are destined
to occupy stations worthy of the character of their
forefathers, in a civilized society. Civilization if properly adapted to them, instead of proving unfriendly to
their nature, is alone calculated to elevate them to the
rank for which Providence appears to have designed
them.

The prospect of the Indian is, however, at this moment overhung by a threatening cloud. Just as their
actions have proved, throughout most of the tribes
within our boundaries, that they are anxious to receive
instruction in letters, arts, and religion ; and just at
the time when one of their nations has adopted a re-
presentative government after the forms of our own.
and is rapidly pursuing the course of improvement,
we are selfish and unprincipled enough seriously to
consider the expediency (not the *justice*) of driving

them out of our territory, and consigning them to a region in the West, where they must lose the advantages they have gained—advantages which we cannot longer question their disposition or capacity to enjoy, and therefore inhumanly propose to wrest from them, with their lands, for ever. Whatever we do in regard to this, and whatever our rulers, either in higher or lower stations, recommend, at the suggestion of interested land-speculators, let us no longer insult humanity and truth by our often repeated professions of friendship to this persecuted race ; and let us not ridicule the Indian for his savage manners, or despise his ignorant simplicity or his faltering speech. His people have justice on their side. The languages they use, in all their countless dialects, may be addressed with more success to Heaven than they have been to their fellow-men ; and the supposed untaught mind of the red man is in possession of at least one important fact—that of our long-continued oppression and injustice—a fact which we may perhaps at some period be willing to obliterate, if possible, even at the sacrifice of the country we have unrighteously ravished from his hands.

Travelling a short time ago in the western part of the state of New-York, I found two Indian men in the stage coach in which I had taken a seat, one of whom, a young man, was accompanied by his wife and infant child. They were remarkably well-behaved, gave no offence, but, on the contrary, appeared kindly disposed ;

and when not engaged in amusing the child, or hushing
its cries, generally maintained a silence, which was
evidently owing to their respect for the company.—
Not having been accustomed to the frequent sight of
persons of their race, I paid strict attention to their
conduct, but perceived nothing improper, forward, or
disagreeable. The look of the female was modest
and intelligent; the child was as playful as if it had
inherited no sorrow. They had spent most of their
lives on a small reservation of Indian soil, in the
midst of white settlements; and were now going
thither, for the last time, to take their little property to
a distant western territory in which a friendly nation
resided, who had furnished them with land. My attention was attracted, while passing a glade in one of
the forest tracts through which our road occasionally
led us, by observing the young Indian point out some
object at a distance through the trees, with a word or
two in his own language, unintelligible to me. I saw
but a few miserable huts in that direction: but having
some curiosity to know why he had taken notice of
them after passing by many splendid buildings in a
town we had left, without giving them a look, he replied that there was a remnant of one of the tribes of
his nation. Those were then the only people he cared
for—and, I suppose for a good reason, because they,
and they only, cared for him.

After riding some distance, and waiting for a shower
to waste itself, while we remained a little while under
a shelter at an inn, the old Indian left our party and
proceeded on foot, even before the rain had quite
ceased. I took an opportunity to make some inquiries

of those that remained, and found it was mere poverty that forced him to walk.

When I had once more seated myself opposite the young Indian family, I could not but reflect that this silent and humble stranger was able to instruct me on subjects of which I was so ignorant as hardly to know how to begin with a question. It was but a few moments before he entered at some length into a description of some of the customs of his nation, in reply to some of my inquiries, and I found myself exceedingly interested as he recounted with what precautions their ancient treaties were guarded and fulfilled, under the old councillors and chiefs, and how solemn and sacred was the trust reposed in those of the nation who guarded the wampum belts, the memorials of these compacts, committed to their charge. I cannot tell with what emotions of compassion mingled with respect and admiration I was filled, when on further inquiry I learned, that one of these old records was carefully preserved in the little pack which his elder companion had taken with him in his lonely and cheerless journey ; and that he would meet hunger, fatigue and distress in silence and content, while he could safely keep this revered deposite, and would sacrifice his life sooner than part with it.

Could some of the monarchs of Europe look down upon this unnoticed chief, this faithful statesman, well might they blush at the broken treaties scattered around them, and the trains of gay courtiers whose flattering professions they know to be so false and so vain.

13*

Caldwell Spring.

THE CONGRESS SPRING.

A SKETCH of the Congress Spring at Saratoga is inserted here, as it is a principal object in the journies of many travellers to the north. The view was taken from a spot a little east of the village street, which passes along in front, on the left leading in the direction of Ballston Springs, (seven miles off,) and on the right passing by the various boarding-houses, hotels, &c. and then proceeding towards Lake George, &c. &c.

The two columns entwined with creeping plants, on the right hand, belong to the piazza of Congress Hall: commonly regarded as the most fashionable place of entertainment. During the travelling season it is the principal resort of the gay, although the United States Hall and the Pavilion are perhaps not behind it in respect to comfort or style of living. Union Hall, another large and good hotel, of somewhat similar appearance, is seen on the opposite side of the street. Mr. Putnam, the father of the present proprietor to that house, is said to have been the discoverer of this valuable spring, which confers on the place its great celebrity. This water, deeply charged with several kinds of salt, was found bubbling up in the bed of the little brook, which now flows in an artificial channel by its side; and it has ever since been pouring an unintermitting stream, for the pleasure of thousands and the benefit of not a few. Most persons after becoming a little accustomed to drinking of the Congress Spring, find it extremely palatable; many prefer the water of this humble rill to the currents that flow from the choicest wine presses of Europe; and for several kinds of diseases is here prepared a safe and effectual remedy.

An interest may well be indulged, by every visiter, in a spot so remarkable as this, which has received from Providence a mysterious supply of a delightful beverage, compounded by nature of several ingredients which the art of the chemist is unable to combine with equal skill and success. Among the variety of company which is annually attracted hither by the celebrity of the waters, the stranger finds much to please him; while those who have before been acquainted with the place, will be reminded of the health restored, or the life preserved by the virtue of the spring, to themselves or their friends.

The low and marshy plain which lies in the foreground of this sketch, abounds in mineral springs, most of which are more or less charged with oxide of iron, and therefore are of a different nature from this. In some places a thin rock is found a little under the surface; but the earth is generally loose, and resembles the little valley in which the springs of Ballston are found. Both of them may have formerly been small lakes, as it is necessary only to suppose the hills united where they approach each other nearest, and where there are appearances of a disrupture in ages past, to see how easily the water which is continually flowing off between them, might have been thrown back so as to overflow a number of acres.

CANAL TRAVELLING.

In the hot season when most travellers are on their
journies, stage coaches are often found uncomfortable, and hotels and inns too often furnish little
real repose to the way-worn stranger. Particularly
does the solitary traveller find himself exposed to evils
of this kind; for he is sometimes condemned to the
poorest coach in the line, and obliged to make one in
those assorted cargoes, which are composed of the
refuse of the travellers, as the horses by which he is
drawn are harnessed together because they are judged
fit for no better company than each other.   The last
bed chamber in a crowded inn, on a side of the house
exposed all the afternoon to a July or August sun, is
not unfrequently his portion at night ; so that, after all,
it may be questioned whether the canal boats, with
their monotony, their comparative sluggishness,
and the republican equality to which they reduce
different grades of society, ought not to be more
generally in good repute, than they are, at least with
some descriptions of travellers.

Perhaps no one ever failed to make such reflections

as these, who has betaken himself to this mode of tra.
velling in the cool of a fine summer morning. He
glides smoothly along, now between green pastures,
orchards and corn.fields ; now round the base of a
hill, or the foot of a rock ; now under the shadow of a
tall forest tree ; occasionally admiring a distant scene
of cultivation, a range of mountains, a thriving village,
or the romantic course of the stream, above which he
is lifted up, by the power of triumphant art and indus.
try. Many persons complain of the want of exercise
in a canal boat; but any one, at setting out for a tour
to Niagara, perhaps designing to see Montreal, Que.
bec, Connecticut River or Boston, before he retires
from the route, will not be impatient to wear out his
strength piecemeal, or insist on feeling in his own
frame the jolting of coach.wheels over every stone on
the western turnpike. Exhilaration will not be want.
ing, if he is wise enough to practise the advice of some
old travellers, to rise with the lark and begin his daily
task before the sun. This should be done whether he
moves by land or water, at all seasons when the weather
is sultry at noon, to allow time for the repose which
should be taken, when it is possible, about mid-day.

A single traveller, on our principal canal routes,
may consult his pleasure in this particular to almost
any extent, as he is not bound to go one furlong
further than he pleases, and can at almost any moment step again into some of the boats continually
passing. If he is only careful to find a good inn, or a
decent boat, at night or meal times, he may occasionally find his account in jumping from a bridge upon
a passing freight boat, and drifting along with a cargo

of flour or a few tons of manufactured articles, till he
reaches some place where he designs again to visit the
shore. The packet-boats, though small in comparison
with the splendid steam-boats on our principal waters,
still present many gratifications to one weary of
crowded stage coaches, dirty roads and burning suns.
First, he has locomotion, even in case of the greatest
crowd : then, he may remain in the shady cabin, or
stand on the more airy deck. The frames which are
hung at night for beds are indeed removed by day ;
but still he may lounge on the long wall-benches, and
fill up memoranda of previous days' rides, or seek
amusement or instruction among the varied authors
which adorn the little library of the boat, or peruse a
few newspapers which usually lie scattered upon the
tables, occasionally looking through the wide and low
windows, at landscapes more beautiful than those which
have been placed in corresponding situations in some
of the splendid steam-boats of New-York.

Artists might well admire some of the scenes we
pass, particularly when the light at morning or evening is favourable. Instead of the broad, barren,
beaten road which the traveller by land has ever in
prospect, before us spreads a cool and level surface of
water, now motionless, now rippling in the breeze, lined
with banks of grass, and overhung with tufts of flowers
or shady forest trees, which are often seen reversed
by reflection in the water below. Masses of verdure
of different hues, form the common foreground of the
picture, interrupted by patches of cultivation, or varied
by mossy rocks or shattered trunks of ancient trees, with
here and there a neighboring log house, or a more

14

costly habitation, indicating the wealth brought by the canal. And sights like these, contemplated as they come up successively to view, when their beauties have been renovated by the dews of night, and while the freshness of the air exhilarates the body and the mind, are capable of administering high gratification, and of arousing those feelings which spontaneously rise amidst the beauty and sublimity of morning scenes.

An experienced traveller will readily admit, that a great portion of the pleasure of a journey may be lost, by choosing unfavourable periods for visiting particular places ; and no doubt many an inexperienced one has been disappointed, at the depreciation of one scene at a second visit, and to find the beauties of another, first seen at a wrong time, either of the day or the year, greatly enhanced. Shakspeare's homely adage :

"All things by season season'd are,"

should never be forgotten on a journey for pleasure. An unlucky traveller, (one of those inconsiderate ones who could vanquish what they call ill fortune if they would exercise a little forethought and care,) will perform the great tour, and return discontented; while one of an opposite character will be able to regale himself and his friends the following winter, with agreeable recollections of the very same objects which the former could not enjoy.

Here and there the canal passes through tracts of country never disincumbered of their primeval forests :

and the traveller occasionally experiences the gratification of a deep and verdant shade from ancient oaks,
pines, hemlocks, elms and ashes, which had never
been startled with the sound of the axe until the canal
came flowing at their roots.   Rocks in some places
rise from its margin, which show curious veins, clouds
and colors, or sparkle with many little points, whose
beauties multiply to the eyes of the mineralogist, as
those of the starry firmament to the astronomer.
How richly endowed is he who can turn an intelligent
eye to objects like these, interesting in themselves,
but capable, when viewed by science, of affording a
new gratification : an attraction of that nature which
accompanies, or rather transports, the learned explo-
rer over mountains and seas, which attended Hum-
boldt far up the Andes, and inspired him while he
managed the pen that recorded the wonders he had
witnessed in nature.

How well may the man of taste and scientific accomplishment reflect, on the eve of a journey, " I
have that magic about me which can transform the
wilderness into a garden, the shadows of the rock
into a cabinet of natural history, and can present to
my vision, even in every blade of grass, every pebble
of the brook, every leaf of the forest, a theatre for the
employment of my thoughts."   How painful is the
void of an empty mind ; how mournful and depressing
are the hours we ignorant ones have to spend in
searching an ill supplied and ill arranged garner, to
satisfy the demands of the intellectual appetite we feel.

The variety of tastes exhibited among travellers is
often amusing : and it has been the lot of many an

observer to remark, that, of a number passing along the same route, scarcely two can be found who seem to have considered, thought upon, or even perceived the same objects : so different are their habits, and the subjects which attract them. But while one is busy in inquiring about the expense of transportation, with an eye to mercantile speculations ; and another visit. ing all the manufactories, mines or quarries that lie in his way ; or while a third converses but on politics, and is interested only concerning candidates, and elec- tions and offices ; an individual may now and then be found whose active and well-stored mind embraces all these, and much more, in its extensive scope. In his thoughts, the close observer will perceive, no wasteful blank occurs. Intervals of listless idleness with other minds, are filled up by him with closely scrutinizing the works which nature has thrown in his way. To him the line of the canal is like the trace drawn upon the touchstone with golden ore : his scientific eye throws out not a little that is useless dross ; though others, less discriminating, might mistake it ; but much remains which is of real value, and appears brighter for the test.

Many of the forest shades and thickets to which this noble work of art affords him access, have here- tofore been as much concealed from eyes like his, as the stones and strata of earth that have been laid open by the plough, or tossed into air with the spade ; and while the latter furnish him with hints concerning the formation of the soil, its nature and capacities : the former offer an exhaustless fund for reflection, on the exuberance of nature's productions. the wonderful manner in which she adapts different plants to different climates, modifies them in conformity with their local situations ; and in all the variety which pervades the branches of science, seems to confess the great truth proclaimed at the creation, that all was formed and arranged on a vast plan, of which the greatest beauty was its benevolence.

These branches of natural history should not be spoken of in comparison with any of those frivolous branches of education, which fashion would fain dignify with the name of accomplishments. Noble in their nature, lofty in their tendency, they are deserving of eulogy on their own merits. Geology embraces Alps and Andes ; botany the inexpressible variety of plants which invest the whole earth. The idle may dislike, and the vain-glorious may despise them ; but the study of these branches of knowledge ought never to be laid aside, while nature continues to present specimens of her wonderful works in the mines and the volcanoes, and changes the face of things every season over the surface of the world : and not until then ought the man of leisure, who has opportunities to learn, cease to blush at his own ignorance when he passes objects like these, without an idea of their natures, their uses, or their names.

LOWER CANADA.

MANY a traveller has felt, and many a future traveller will feel, what I experienced the first day I
crossed the northern boundary of the United States,
and entered Lower Canada. Instead of finding, as
we are apt to expect, marks of a hyperborean region :
the pure sky, the rich vegetation, the fertile fields,
and the crowded population, together with the heat,
which is sometimes oppressive in the summer months,
might lead us to fancy we had reached a tropical climate. The traveller's route, in a large majority of
cases, lies along part of that wide and unvarying level
that borders the St. Lawrence, to which the original
colonists confined their settlements, and over which
their descendants have extended their innumerable
fields and whitewashed cottages, and where they ad-
here to the soil as pertinaciously as to the language
and customs of their ancestors.

Any one acquainted with the rich appearance of a
fertile country cultivated in detail for ages, by a people of simple habits ; and who knows the peculiar

beauty of the face of nature, in regions where the vegetation is rapid in proportion to the shortness of the summer, may form some idea beforehand of what he is to see in Lower Canada. Others, however, can never entertain an adequate conception of it, until they ascend the mountain of Montreal, and take a glance at the scene below. It may be seriously inquired whether a scene of a similar nature, equal in extent and beauty, is any where to be found within the compass of our common American tours. Compared with that from Mount Holyoke, it is inferior in fertility and variety of natural surface, as well as in the moral associations connected with the state and refinements of society ;—but in point of extent, both of country and population, which it comprehends, as well as with regard to the size and rapidity of the mighty river which passes beneath the eye, the importance of the great city lying at the feet, the novelties which the curious mind may wish to search out in a foreign land, the vast regions which the waters beneath us have already visited, and the remote and interesting countries with which they afford a direct communication :—on considerations like these the sight we are enjoying has a superiority to boast over almost every other scene the American traveller is offered for his gratification and delight. The pleasure he here enjoys is much enhanced by the contrast he perceives between a level district, highly cultivated, and extending to the horizon, with the bold and wild features, the rocky and barren mountains, which he has lately admired, in passing the length of Lake Champlain.

This commanding elevation rises at a spot where the St. Lawrence, after having rushed and foamed over the last of the series of Rapids, to which it is introduced after parting from Lake Ontario, first subsides into a placid current. It is here that the dauntless boatman discovers the smooth surface which relieves him from anxiety, if not from apprehension; and where many a birch canoe has been moored in safety, after the countless dangers of the upper navigation. The spectator on one hand may trace some of those milk-white rapids where the current wages war with the skill and industry of man in the summer season, and with the masses of ice by which winter so often in vain endeavours to connect the opposite shores. Before him extends a portion of that valley which reaches almost to Quebec, and may be supposed to have been formed by an ancient lake, a sister of Ontario and Champlain, until the current cut a deeper passage through the mountains in that vicinity. On this extensive surface—uniform except where it is interrupted by a few distant and solitary peaks—are collected the descendants of the old French colonists, who were the first representatives of Europe in this region. Looking down upon them as we do from this height, we feel an interest both in them and the soil for each other's sake—an interest which, though it may receive some checks on minute acquaintance, will, on the whole, increase rather than diminish, during our stay in Lower Canada.

The Canadian husbandman has labored silently along with little notice from the world, for the last two cen-

turies; and seems likely to pursue the same unvarying course for an equal period to come, unless some
unforeseen accident should occur, to give a new direction to his faculties. Like the small but powerful
animal which assists him in his labors, he persists in
preserving the form, the step, and the trappings of his
ancestors, content with their simple food, their hardy
industry and their plain enjoyments, without wishing
for the distinction which a loftier bearing might confer,
or once raising a question of what might be the result of his breaking the gait of his ancestors.—
Whoever has been rowed through the rapids of the
St. Lawrence by a band of Canadian boatmen, and,
had heard their cheerful boat-song: or passed along
its banks on a summer evening, and seen the happy
family circles which assemble at the doors of the
little farm-houses after the labors of the day, will ever
remember them with feelings of pleasure. It may
indeed be doubted, whether a race of people can be
found, better calculated by nature to appear to a
stranger light-hearted and gay. They retain much of
the vivacity of the French character; and the vari-
ation of temperature, the aspects of nature, and the
condition of the inhabitants which the seasons produce, increase by contrast the enjoyments of all.—
When we visit them, they are in the midst of their
fields, which are covered with bright and fresh vegetation, so green, so luxuriant, and so transitory, that
the inhabitants seem to regard them with almost as
much surprise as ourselves, who are accustomed to
think of Canada only as the region that supplies us
with the sharp, freezing winds of winter.

When we come to form a more intimate acquaintance with the people, although their character presents some excellent materials for improvement, we
find that their gaiety and happiness are not deeply
grounded, or substantial in their foundations, but that
the intellectual waste is still more extensive, lasting,
and lamentable than the natural one in those months
which are condemned to the rigour of winter. In this
view we find much to regret in their condition, and little
to hope for in their prospects. They will doubtless
preserve the plain, industrious habits, the cheerful and
friendly deportment, the conciliating manners, the
smiling faces, and the contented hearts which now
strongly recommend them to the feelings of a stranger; but by what means they are ever to be raised to
the respectable and dignified rank, the higher enjoyments and more estimable character to which so many
other people are now aspiring, is a question perhaps
very difficult to answer, but certainly very natural to
ask, and very well worthy of examination.

Very little has been published in England relating
to the inhabitants of Lower Canada : a people, who
after having been under the British government for
above seventy years, are apparently as yet little known
to those of England, or to their near neighbours in
the United States. They differ in the important
points of language, religion, origin, and manners ;
and are led to believe that they differ also in interests.
The Lower Canadian feels no common bond of union
with us ; there is, indeed, apparently no neutral
ground on which he can meet any of those with whom
he is sometimes brought into contact against his will :

and there seems to be not a moment in which he can lay aside his feelings and declare an armistice with his prejudices and antipathies.

Every stranger from the United States, on entering the district of which we are speaking, must be struck with the sudden change in the aspect of society, and the physiognomy as well as the language of the people, which takes place in almost as great a degree, and with as sudden a gradation, as that which is observed on crossing the British channel from Dover to Calais. But it is not every traveller who has the disposition and the opportunity to ascertain to what causes this phenomenon is attributable. In regard to many improvements in the useful arts, and, it is to be hoped, in their intellectual condition generally, the common people of France have made more progress than this scion from their stock, since the period of its foreign engrafting. Indeed, those best acquainted with the Lower Canadians, seem to agree in considering them as having remained stationary in these respects, and as not having advanced, in any important particular, in two centuries. In the appearance of their fields the passenger is reminded of modes and practices, implements and processes, alluded to in old and musty books ; and discovers that doctrines in agriculture are in vogue and application, which have been exploded even in the country from which they were introduced. The Canada thistle, which seems to threaten the rooting out of every useful plant, instead of being itself exterminated or checked by some judicious treatment, is cherished and extended by the ancient and stubborn practice of long fallows, to which every cultivated tract is condemned, after yielding a few crops of one species, under a belief that this is the only way by which fertility can be restored. It is to no purpose, so far as the Canadian farmer is concerned, that his near southern neighbours till their land in a more rational and profitable manner: he seems to regard every thing they do with distorted eyes, or rather to remain in wilful ignorance of them and their affairs.

The cause is not difficult of discovery: the traveller who has passed through any part of the adjacent states, looks in vain among the Canadians for the newspapers, and the volumes, however few, which are almost invariably found among the necessary furniture even of the log-houses of the new settlers in the former. Those objects there indicate to the observer the extent to which the supplies ramify from the great current of intelligence, and are apportioned to every neighbourhood, and almost every individual. But here is nothing of the kind. The current, so abundant where it flows, runs but to the boundary. The frontier line is the shore of this sea, over which the waters cannot pass; and it would seem as if nothing, unless some great convulsion, could ever even sprinkle the barren sand with its spray. The people of the United States, ever since the first settlement of their country, have been assiduous in obtaining and diffusing the useful knowledge promulged in the land of their origin. But the Canadians, although their language might have served as an easy and natural vehicle for the importation of every thing that it has given currency to in enlightened France, has performed only the negative and the opposite task of excluding every thing English. It was on account of the rapid improvement of the one, and the stationary condition of the other, that the American Revolution found no materials to work upon among the Canadians. They acted differently, because they felt and thought differently; and their difference of character is doubtless owing to the system under which they are educated. That system is in its material points the same which rules in Italy, and Spain, and which reduces the inhabitants of those countries so nearly to a level.

Some would fain have us believe, that there is something naturally deficient in the intellect of the Canadians; but when placed in situations where their powers of mind or body are called into exercise, they are found to cast off their reputed inactivity and stupidity. On the dangerous St. Lawrence, and along the upper lakes, the Canadian voyageur combats against cold and hunger with firmness, temper, and success, and rivals the Indian himself in the dexterous management of the light canoe; while in the inhospitable regions of the north, his faithfulness and hardihood equal those of the generous dog, which is often his only companion.

It is no want of natural capacity, energy or feeling which restricts them so precisely within the bounds marked out by their ancestors: it is the imperfections and errors of the system under which they live. They are ignorant and superstitious: to them the acquisition of knowledge is forbidden, and as effectually cut off, as if they inhabited the most unenlightened regions in Eu-

rope ; and among a population which circumstances,
hereafter to be named, shut up from foreign admixture,
the results are surprisingly similar, and indeed, in the
main points, identically the same.   This remark is not
intended to apply exclusively to the country people, the
cultivators of the soil along the St. Lawrence ; but
to a large portion of those who inhabit the cities :
although among many individuals of the upper classes
some knowledge, liberality and justness of sentiment,
have unavoidably crept in.   In the towns the great
obstacle of a separate language is partly overthrown
by the intercourse of society, prejudices are softened, and the world is so far presented and regarded
in a new view.   In the cities and their environs the
stranger is often attracted by the neat and elegant
mansions of Canadian gentlemen, the hereditary seigneurs of large tracts of land, or those who owe their
fortunes to their industry, where the architecture, the
system of tillage, and the prevailing aspect of things,
so strongly marked with the peculiarities of the country, yet bear the encouraging traces of valuable
modern innovations : while those who have an opportunity to witness their manners and to hear their opinions, will be gratified to observe that changes still
more remarkable and important are going on in their
minds.   As yet, however, the influence of these
changes appears not to have reached the other classes ;
but as the interest recently excited among all on political matters, naturally encourages more general intercourse, it is probable that, by its means, the improv-
ing spirit may by degrees be extended.   A great deal

is first to be done, before any material change can be effected in the population.

Although limited to an inconsiderable amount, it would seem to a common traveller that the number of the French Lower Canadians must be five times greater than it is; for they thickly line the banks of the St. Lawrence from above Montreal to Quebec: and from the commanding height near the former, their innumerable little white dwellings are seen scattered over an extensive and highly cultivated region, the limit of which the eye cannot discover, and which he may look for in vain for many hours, from the swiftest steam-boat. But besides these, there are few extensive settlements of these people; and if the stranger were to penetrate into the country in almost any direction, he would soon find himself in the forests, or on the confines of some of the numerous Scotch or English settlements, which abound in many parts of the interior.

The first traits that strike the traveller in the aspect of this people, are their equality and contentment. The latter is attributable to their ignorance, if it exists in the degree commonly supposed. They have no inducement to wander from home, and they see nothing with which to compare themselves. As for the equality existing in their society, it is not that which prevails in the neighbouring states, which is the effect of an universal diffusion of education, and a system of general encouragement to every useful exertion: but it is that revolting equality produced by an universal depression of the intellect. Men are in such a case ranked more by the offensive and defensive capacities which nature or circumstance has given them ; and like the animals in the woods, are reduced to one degraded scale.

With regard to the obstacles to be removed before any general improvement can be introduced, some idea may be formed of them by the mention of a few. The priests have such influence among them, that their power must be overcome or eluded before the means of useful instruction can be furnished to the people. Their ears could not be more effectually closed against a teacher, if they were the inhabitants of Madrid, Venice, or Rome. They are taught to give implicit obedience to their priests, and their priests watch night and day, (some of them no doubt in ignorant sincerity,) against the invasions of useful knowledge : and as nothing but the frontier requires guarding, such assiduity does not fail of success. As yet the priests have had little to fear from internal foes : the uncertainty of land tenures, together with the numerous and vexatious taxes to which every possessor of real estates is subject, has thus far operated as a successful barrier against the emigrations of those restless and enterprising people who inhabit the country on the south. The Lower Canadian farmer, claiming a title to his land under one of the Seigneurs who possess the country by large tracts, may be for years in doubt of his legal right, as it may have been exposed to forfeiture by various negligencies or informalities, sometimes beyond the sagacity of a skilful lawyer fully to ascertain ; and even a seigneur was not long since ejected from his purchased estate and

15*

title, after a possession of thirty years. The certificates of regular sale by authority of the courts, though regarded as the most satisfactory documents, are by no means unquestionable ; and thus a death-blow is struck at all encouragement of foreign settlers, the value and improvement of the soil effectually checked, and the moral benefits of introducing a portion of a better population entirely prevented.* Exertions have been made to extend to them the means of instruction, but hitherto without success. Plans are proposed to ascertain and record the titles and transfers of land, which may soon be adopted by the Provincial Government, and can hardly fail to meet the approbation of the British king.

Among the arts of life, as practised by them, we find rather the marks of instinct than the evidence of reason. They carry with them to the grave the customs and the opinions which their fathers and grandfathers received by tradition ; for being denied the right of questioning on matters of religion, why should they be able to judge on those of vastly inferior interest ? But while they go on, with persevering though almost fruitless industry, to turn up their soil with the implements of the Gothic ages, science accompanies our husbandmen to the field, lightens their labors and doubles their harvests. For them the man who

* It was recently stated before a committee of the British House of Commons, that the boundary line alone divided acres worth one shilling in Canada and twelve shillings in New-York.

traverses distant seas and unknown countries spends
his strength for nought; as does he who gives himself to investigations in any branch of the sciences :
while every traveller and every philosopher devotes
to the advantage of our countrymen some portion of
his labours, the useful results of which are dispensed
to all by the never-resting press. No new region is
discovered but we mark its position on our maps ; no
improvement is made in the arts but it is brought into
practice in our workshops ; no new star is discovered
in the sky, but it is proclaimed in all our cottages,
where ingenuity ponders upon it with unshackled
mind, piety receives another ray of light from heaven,
and knowledge marks it as another stage on a journey
which is not only delightful but interminable.

A little sketch is introduced to accompany this chapter, presenting an assemblage of objects characteristic of some parts of the St. Lawrence. A low shore
like this is seen almost every where on the journey
from Montreal to Quebec, and distant mountains, like
that of Belle Isle, (which is drawn in outline,) are
occasionally seen in the vicinity of the former city.
The church represented is that of Boucherville : and
the dwellings seen in different places are those small
houses, of one story, whitewashed, sometimes formed
of logs, with their thatched barns, which so thickly
line the banks, but extend not far in the interior.—
The birch canoes, of which a specimen is given, are

used in the navigation of the upper lakes, principally in the fur trade carried on by the Hudson's Bay Company. Some of them are capable of containing two tons, and are safe boats under the care of expert Indian or Canadian rowers, but are almost inevitably overset by one unaccustomed to the management of them.— The mountain introduced here in outline is out of place, being, in fact, on the other side of the river.

Entrance of the Highlands.

THE HIGHLANDS.

It seldom happens that such fine scenery as that of the Highlands on the Hudson River is easily accessible, and placed on a route necessarily visited by a great number of travellers. The annexed sketch may give a general idea of the form of the mountains which mark the southern extremity of this romantic pass.— As the stranger approaches in one of those rapid steam-boats which are continually plying between New-York and Albany, the breadth of the river is suddenly contracted to a very narrow space ; and the channel makes a short bend, which leaves him in uncertainty concerning its direction. A few moments more, and he finds himself at the point whence our view was taken, with his eye limited to a few near and lofty elevations, rude, rough, and almost uninhabited, whence the breezes that are felt a little lower down the stream are often excluded, and where they are sometimes forced through the narrow chasm with redoubled force. He has already passed the spots where the old works of defence were erected, that stood to guard the stream above against the enemy in the Revolutionary War. The two forts, Montgomery and Clinton, stood like champions in the front ranks in ancient times ; while the defences at Stony Point on one side of the river, and Verplank's on the other, just at the point where the stream contracts itself, stood prepared, with the best means in the possession of our officers, to second the defence of this highly important pass. Among the well-known events in the history of the campaign of 1777, was the capture of these posts by the British, whose numbers over-powered our own resolute but feeble forces, and held for a time the fortresses in these mountains, though the speedy defeat of Burgoyne rendered their tempo-rary successes worthless.

TRAVELLING TO GOOD PURPOSE.

AFTER a return from our journey, when we find ourselves once safely restored again to our homes; when the trials and the pleasures of the way are alike passed, and we are beginning to mingle again in a more unvarying round of well-known scenes, the important question is not what we have enjoyed, and whether weather and circumstances, companions and objects, have been such as we would have preferred, but what knowledge have we obtained which may be applied to some useful purpose.

Some individuals, among the numerous travellers for pleasure, may be found with something like a method laid down to pursue : but the greater part appear to be influenced only by their present gratification, in the objects to which they direct their attention at different stages of their journies ; and not a few of them we find every season traversing the country, at all rates and in all directions, passing some great objects unobserved, suddenly changing their course when in the neighbourhood of others, surprised with discoveries which the very newspapers are weary of describ-

ing, and finally carrying home with them nothing
distinct, interesting, or useful. This is to abuse travelling. The great features of our country, the leading events of its history, and the details of its natural
productions ; our arts of life, our condition and habits,
are now so easily accessible in popular publications,
that foreigners themselves are ashamed to travel without some preparation by reading ; and our own citizens have sometimes been hushed into silence while
listening to the intelligent remarks of those who have
a right to seek of them instruction. This is said with
the hope that it may be useful. Our own travellers
have too much given in to the fashion of carrying
foreign novels and poems with them to read on their
journies—a habit, which, as far as it prevails, has its
origin in taste at least ill-timed, if not in pedantry of
a very mistaken kind.

Instead of wishing to see the world through a fan-
cied medium, the rational traveller wishes to view it
as it is. He takes with him such books as contain
necessary information in a compact and convenient
form ; and, at setting out, endeavours to divest his
mind of all prejudice, as well as to prepare his feelings to slide easily over the little trials he must expect,
determined neither to fail of the enjoyments which
lie before him by extravagant anticipations, nor to
diminish them unnecessarily by unfortunate compari-
sons. After his return he may recount what pleasure
he has derived from the journey, for the purpose of
better planning a succeeding one ; but his reflection
should be chiefly directed to reviewing and arranging
the knowledge he has acquired, and considering how

he may apply it in the most advantageous manner.

To one of peculiarly retired habits and diffident feelings,(many such there are among our travellers,) it may afford much gratification to reflect, that he has well employed his time, has witnessed scenes of an interesting nature, and laid up in his memory subjects for pleasing and useful reflection. The more active and practical philanthropist will have discovered with delight how many individuals of a similar character his country contains; how multitudes are devoting their exertions to the good of the young and the old, the stranger, the fatherless, and the widow, in the various modes in which charity is capable of being dispensed by man; and view with joy the opportunities the good possess in our day, of obtaining and communicating useful knowledge, and of proposing and enlisting in philanthropic projects, where a common spirit has created a unity of interest, and broken down the old obstacles which formality had thrown between. What an exhilarating reflection it is, that the most obscure and friendless individual in the United States has but to ask for the bible, or the most remote hamlet have but to inquire for instruction in the best modes of educating their children, and the mails will bear the request through their various channels to the hand of some benevolent personage an hundred or a thousand miles distant, who, with a glowing heart, will soon despatch them the prize they desire. Females, in more than one instance, occupy prominent positions among these benefactors. Cold must be the heart that does not feel affected at the recollection of such

16

individuals, and their deeds of charity, after the various objects of the journey have passed from the eye. Many there are who cannot resist the desire to imitate them in their appropriate spheres ; and could those who furnish the example, but know the extent to which it influences others—could they see how their doctrines and practice are put to the test in the retired hamlets of New-England, the mixed villages of the West, and even the plantations of the South, overshadowed by so dark a veil of ignorance—they might be encouraged to redouble, if it were possible, their diligence in action and their gratitude for success.

If in the course of reflection which has been imperfectly sketched in the descriptions of a few scenes in the preceding chapters, any thing should have been found that appears judicious and appropriate, to an intelligent mind, future travellers will find abundance of other scenes where similar sentiments and considerations may be naturally suggested; and if among the subjects which have been touched upon, any useful suggestion should be found, which may before have arisen to the view of any individual, he will reflect with pleasure on the coincidence by which more than one person has been struck by the same idea.

He who has at any period of his life ever travelled to good purpose, is very apt to evince that fact, though unsuspectingly and without design, to the sagacious and attentive observer. The wider the range he has enjoyed, the greater the opportunities he has had to learn by that most satisfactory mode—personal observation, the more evident is the effect upon his cha-

racter. This scrutiny has heretofore been most directed to those who have visited foreign countries, for
objects of pleasure or improvement. While the wild,
the extravagant, and the uninstructed have been observed to bring home with them little more than their
own ignorance and the prejudices or vices of others,
and to exhibit during their lives, their deficiencies and
circumscribed opinions in an unfavorable relief; those
who have made better use of their advantages have
carried with them to their latest days more extended
views, more unprejudiced minds, with a large and continually increasing fund of valuable information, and
habits of industry and simplicity of life ; and these
facts the man of a similar character scarcely fails to
discover and admire in their ordinary manners and de-
meanour.

An individual whom I have now in my recollection,
but whom it is unnecessary to name, might be adduced
as an example pretty well corresponding with such a
description. Nature gave him so good sense, and
education did so much to improve his mind and to cultivate the native good feelings of his heart, that extraordinary genius would have appeared in his case almost a superfluous boon. Looking back upon a highly
distinguished family, and around him upon a rising
and happy one, with taste and philanthropy to stimu-
late, and an abundant fortune to sustain, he devoted a few months to traversing some of the most
attractive countries of Europe ; and as his eyes fixed
upon every thing which seemed calculated to be
taken home with advantage, and his practical mind
had the capacity of discriminating with readiness and

clearness between the useful and the useless, he was in possession of a stock of information on his return of an amount not easily to be computed, and precisely of that description which he was best able to bring, and I doubt not will be able extensively to diffuse, with great public benefit.

His house, which is more than ever open to hospitality, not only rests the weary and refreshes the stranger—names he has learnt the meaning of by experience in foreign lands—but delights the man of taste, by its choice selections from transatlantic cabinets and libraries, gratifies and instructs the good, (the highest praise a house can bear,) by offering to them the projects of benevolence, and the master productions of those who think and live for mankind.— Hardly a person now leaves that mansion without reflections of the most pleasing nature ; and while its master is indulging in the agreeable sensations enjoyed by a generous man diffusing the rights of hospitality, the guest retires, admiring at the advantages of travel, and contemplating the individual who has had the good sense to turn it to the best account.

In his grounds, his furniture, and his dress, you spy no prominent trait of foreign fashions. In conversation his tongue neither betrays familiarity with foreign languages, nor affects contempt for his own. He is not profuse of insincere professions because they are so in Paris, nor does he applaud immorality because it prevails in Venice or Naples ; he does not plead fashion as an excuse for folly like many of his predecessors, nor impress freethinking into his conversation because those he has met with in Europe have

done it. He would regard it as an unwarrantable
vanity in him to place his still limited knowledge of
foreign modes in opposition to the general opinions
of those he respects, and a mark of contempt towards
the country and customs of his ancestors, to dis-
countenance their fashions and their manners. In
more momentous concerns he is bound to the prevailing sound sentiments of his native country by higher
considerations : for instead of being turned mad, like
some, by a very little knowledge, he has acquired
enough to be more sedate and decided than before.—
The ignorance, misery, and profligacy, which it was
too often his lot to meet with while abroad, would have
made him personally vain of being an American, had
not his better judgment taught him rather to be
grateful than proud, and to acknowledge the sources
of his blessings by practising those virtues to
which they are due. His object appears to be, to
introduce among his countrymen such new ideas on
practical subjects, and such institutions, as he knows
might prove useful to the public ; and he studies to
present them to the minds of others in an unobtrusive
manner, and to lay them before their unbiassed judgment, unimpeded by any obstacles which the self-
conceit or dictatorial forwardness of less sensible men
might have accompanied them with to their own defeat.

A portrait like this may now be more appropriately
applied to travellers of intelligence within our limits,
than it could have been a few years ago ; for in that
time we have made great progress in various branches
of improvement, and the country presents more to
learn, and offers a thousand more channels for the

16*

acquisition of knowledge, as well as a far greater va‑
riety of ways for applying it with effect. To what
extent travelling may be made useful, those alone are
capable of deciding who have been assiduous in con‑
verting it to advantage in all the variety of modes of
which it is capable. It is certain, however, that the
annual excursions and tours made by so many fami‑
lies in the northern parts of this country might be ren‑
dered much more agreeable, and much more useful
than they usually are, by a little forethought and
method. To the elder individuals the commencement
of a journey offers opportunities for adminstering to
the instruction as well as enjoyment of the younger.
The latter are in a happy frame of mind, with their
faculties ready to seize upon every thing new with
avidity, and well prepared to receive lessons from
their parents, who have conferred upon them the high
gratification they are beginning to enjoy. The judi‑
cious parent has already suggested to them the nature
of some of the principal objects they are to observe,
and unconsciously to them, by representations made,
or by opinions expressed, has laid the foundation on
which their future observations are to be built. How
important is it that the parent should not have over‑
rated trifles, or undervalued or omitted objects of real
importance, as the infant mind so easily receives a
wrong bias, and is very apt to regard in an erroneous
view, through a whole life, what has been at first pre‑
sented in an improper light.

One of the most interesting objects that can be pre‑
sented on a journey, is that of an affectionate mother
directing the attention of her little family to scenes

through which they pass : and an acute observer would hardly wish a better opportunity to form an opinion of the intelligence and judgment of a parent, than that which is afforded by listening to the train of remarks on such an occasion. Impressions thus communicated to the young are almost sure to be permanent. In their future travels they will select similar objects for their attention, and similar reflections will be suggested to their minds.

One mode in which young travellers, as well as older ones, will find it easy to retain what they see and think in their recollection, is by regularly noting it down in a diary. The journals of the young have often been ridiculed, and generally with a degree of justice when they have been thought worthy of the public eye ; but this consideration should not be permitted, so far as it has been, to put diaries out of countenance. The observing parent will perceive with pleasure how much the child and the youth are stimulated to accurate remark by the consciousness that they are to record in writing something of what they see. After their return from the journey also, the family circle may derive great gratification from retracing their steps, and renewing their reflections, over the little pages of such early essays. The remarks will not be new, but many of them will be original in the little individual who made them, and who will as well merit the applause of acuteness, good taste, or benevolent feelings as if he had been the first in the world to express them. Such he often considers himself in such cases ; and he will find it a disheartening thing if his best attempts are treated with derision, and if what he regards as his most successful efforts to employ his time well are condemned for being *trite* and *true.*

Parents too would find their advantage in noting down facts and thoughts during their travels, as subjects on which to enlarge by the winter fire-side, to the little listeners of the family circle. Nor is this useful practice to be confined to them. Every individual has it in his power to contribute to the convenience, enjoyment, or information of others in some similar manner. Travelling has already conferred much enjoyment, greatly extended a knowledge of the country, softened strong prejudices, tamed many asperities, and strengthened the bonds between different states. All this it has done, and much more it is capable of doing.

APPENDIX.

THE WHITE MOUNTAINS.

SINCE the chapter on the White Mountains passed through the press, permission has been kindly furnished to publish the following letter written to a friend, which describes with precision the effects of the great storm, as they appeared about a year ago. The writer, who is a gentleman of correct and cultivated taste, and has had opportunities enjoyed by few to witness celebrated natural scenes, both in America and Europe, hesitates not to declare, that the devastation of that region, originally so wild and sublime, produced such feelings in his mind as he had never before experienced. The reader may be better able to participate in them, after perusing what he has written in his own words.

In speaking of the appearance of the mountain which is represented in the sketch inserted at page 59, he remarks as follows :—

"The structure of it was discernible on all parts,

and a great number of rocks are exposed. Indeed all the surface is of rocks or gravel. The trees were all, *literally* swept away. There may, perhaps, be some slight shrubbery, either left, or beginning to peep through the gravel; but in May the season was not far enough advanced to allow the feeble twigs which might exist to put forth leaves sufficient to give any appearance of verdure. The slides appeared like deep grooves, lately made by the violence of torrents of water, carrying with them irresistible masses of granite; some taking their whole course to the valley—others arrested by their own bulk or number, in the midst of their career.

"Some of the gulfs are fifty feet deep, and as wide: some, I have no doubt, much wider and deeper, and half filled with countless trunks of trees.

"The slides on the longer and less precipitate descents, seen at a distance from different positions, were, I have no doubt, much broader, from their having time, in moving so far, to spread. I saw some, which, instead of cutting their way into the mountain, had piled up what seemed a mighty work of art—an immense turnpike-road made of rocks alone (without a particle of earth,) from the size of a cannon-ball to that of a moderate sized-house.

"The general surface of the mountains which suffered by the slides is not craggy; except where heavy masses of rock stood out. The gravel and earth seemed well flattened by the sweeping waters that had rushed over them.

"I will give you an opinion I have formed as to the cause of the slides, at least to some extent; and also of what will be the consequences in future to the public road through the Notch. I do not know how much it is worthy of attention; others, perhaps, will have other views and other theories. Several years of extreme drought had preceded the one in which the catastrophe took place. The rains came on with great violence, and continued for some weeks almost uninterrupted; and at last the water fell like a cataract. Then the surface of the mountain gave way, being filled with water, and rushed from above. This, I have no doubt, would have happened on the higher mountains, where the trees were few, short, and stunted, and the soil thin; and when once the upper part, with a few rocks, had begun to move, the accumulation would become irresistible, and the velocity increase at every tremendous leap; and in long distances the ruin would be widely spread.

"But on those mountains which form the *Pass*, as their summits are not elevated above the region even of very strong vegetation, (for when I visited the place more than twenty years ago, they were clothed to the tops with very heavy timber,) I do not believe any very important slide would have taken place, had not the forest trees been destroyed by repeated fires.— Their very roots, being dead, served now to loosen the soil to which they had once given tenacity. The depredations had begun just before I was first there.— There had been a fire, by accident or design, from the Notch House up to the passage out, which had been seen quite at Portland, and *heard* at Lancaster. The trees, like giants, still stood—their trunks black and terrific—like an army of infernal warriors, ascending from the gloomy abyss, to attack the spirits that lived in light above the Mountains.

"Whether there be any thing in the opinion I have expressed, I know not. You have it for what it is worth. I should like to know what you think of it.— I think the Notch will ever be subject to the same in-cidents, and the road filled up every two or three years."

THE END.